LIFE AND LABOUR IN RURAL ENGLAND, 1760-1850

Pamela Horn

MACMILLAN
EDUCATION

First published 1987

Published by
MACMILLAN EDUCATION LTD
Houndmills, Basingstoke, Hampshire RG21 2XS
and London
Companies and representatives
throughout the world

Typeset by
Wessex Typesetters
(Division of The Eastern Press Ltd)
Frome, Somerset

Printed in Hong Kong

British Library Cataloguing in Publication Data
Horn, Pamela
  Life and labour in rural England
  1760–1850.——(Context and commentary)
  1. England——Rural conditions
  I. Title   II. Series
  942'.009734   HN398.E5
ISBN 0–333–37584–X
ISBN 0–333–37585–8 Pbk

Contents

Acknowledgements

I should like to thank all those who have assisted in the preparation of this book, either by providing material or in other ways. My thanks are due, in particular, to Lady Lucas for permission to quote from the Wrest Park papers at Bedford Record Office.

I have received much help from the staff at the libraries and record offices in which I have worked. These include the Bodleian Library, Oxford; the British Library; the Public Record Office; the Museum of English Rural Life, Reading and the County Record Offices for Bedfordshire and Buckinghamshire.

I should also like to express my appreciation to Professor Arthur Pollard, the general editor, for his encouragement and advice.

Finally, as always, I owe a great debt of gratitude to my family – particularly to my husband, who has assisted me in so many ways.

Pamela Horn

List of Plates

1. The drawing room of a well-to-do eighteenth-century landed family by John Harden. Mother and daughters are occupying themselves by reading and writing.
   Photograph © Abbot Hall Art Gallery, Kendal.
2. *Reapers*, an engraving by George Stubbs, 1791. Even the womenfolk were expected to lend a hand with the harvest, which was the focal point of the farming year.
   Photograph © Trustees of the British Museum.
3. *Labourers*, as employed on Lord Torrington's estate at Southill, from an engraving by George Stubbs, 1789.
   Photograph © Trustees of the British Museum.
4. Machine-breaking and the firing of ricks were two of the most frightening aspects of the 'Swing' riots.
   Photograph © Pamela Horn.
5. The 'Swing' riots of 1830.
   Photograph © Museum of English Rural Life, Reading.
6. Children employed in a mid-nineteenth-century agricultural gang in the Eastern Counties. For some of the overworked and ill-fed youngsters the task proved too much.
   Photograph © Pamela Horn.

Editor's Preface

J.H. Plumb has said that 'the aim of (the historian) is to understand men both as individuals and in their social relationships in time. "Social" embraces all of man's activities – economic, religious, political, artistic, legal, military, scientific – everything, indeed, that affects the life of mankind.' Literature is itself similarly comprehensive. From Terence onwards writers have embraced his dictum that all things human are their concern.

It is the aim of this series to trace the interweavings of history and literature, to show by judicious quotation and commentary how those actually working within the various fields of human activity influenced and were influenced by those who were writing the novels, poems and plays within the several periods. An attempt has been made to show the special contribution that such writers make to the understanding of their times by virtue of their peculiar imaginative 'feel' for their subjects and the intensely personal angle from which they observe the historical phenomena that provide their inspiration and come within their creative vision. In its turn the historical evidence, besides and beyond its intrinsic importance, serves to 'place' the imaginative testimony of the writers.

The authors of the several volumes in this series have sought to intermingle history and literature in the conviction that the study of each is enhanced thereby. They have been free to adopt their own approach within the broad general pattern of the series. The topics themselves have sometimes also a particular slant and emphasis. Commentary, for instance, has had to be more detailed in some cases than in others. All the contributors to the series are at one, however, in the belief (at a time when some critics would not only divorce texts from their periods but even from their authors) that literature is the creation of actual men and women, actually living in an identifiable set of historical circumstances, themselves both the creatures and the creators of their times.

ARTHUR POLLARD

'In the "dark ages", when I was a boy, country labourers' wives used to spin the wool, and knit the stockings and gloves that were wanted in the family. My grandmother knitted stockings for me after she was blind. Farmers' wives and daughters, and servant maids, were spinning, reeling, carding, knitting, or at something or other of that sort, whenever the work of the farm-house did not demand them. . . . Rural affairs leave not a day, not an hour, unoccupied and without its cares, its promises, and its fruitions. The seasons, which wait for no man; the weather, which is no respecter of persons, and which will be what it will be, produce an habitual looking forward, and make the farmer provident, whatever might have been his natural disposition. The farmer's cares are pleasing cares. His misfortunes can seldom be more than lessons. His produce consists of things wanted by all mankind.'

The Autobiography of William Cobbett (1967) ed. by William Reitzel, pp.15, 234-35. (Cobbett was born at Farnham, Surrey in 1763 and died in 1835.)

1 Change in the Countryside

Although the deep and seemingly irreparable split between urban and rural viewpoints is comparatively recent, a distinction between town and country is, of course, as old as literature and recorded history. . . . Often, as almost any restoration comedy demonstrates, the town is regarded as the ultimate in wit and civilized amusement while the country is the home of vulgar, ignorant, and drunken boors. But the advantage is even more frequently on the side of the rural. Indeed 'the Countries sweet simplicity,' as Herrick calls it, is continually being contrasted disparagingly with Tennyson's 'dust and din and steam of town', and around this basic opposition develops a number of convenient literary myths. Prominent among these, of course, is the myth of rural innocence.

W.J. Keith, *The Rural Tradition* (1975), pp.1; 6.

The Changing Countryside and Industrialisation

The years from 1760 to 1850 were to prove among the most momentous in the history of the English countryside, for it was during this period that agriculture and its associated trades ceased to dominate the national economy in the way they had done from time immemorial. Instead they were overtaken by the products of urban manufacturing and the mining industry. As late as 1811 agriculture, forestry and fishing contributed more than a third of the gross national product – more than any other sector – but by 1851 that share had dwindled to about a fifth and it was manufacturing, mining and building which now held the lead.

In the final quarter of the eighteenth century northern industrialism started to challenge the pre-eminence of the landed interest, as the new water or steam-powered textile mills began to make their contribution. Elsewhere country people were drawn into the manufacturing process by the expansion of traditional industries like framework knitting, nailmaking and woollen clothmaking, conducted within the home or small workshop. This expansion of what has been labelled proto-industrialism was particularly characteristic of the first half of the period. Thereafter, in the early nineteenth century, the growth of the large production unit, be it factory or workshop, undermined and eventually destroyed most of these domestic arrangements, the cottage clothmaking industry being one of the earliest victims. Elizabeth Gaskell in the opening paragraphs of her biography of Charlotte Brontë emphasised the impact of such developments upon the landscape of one district affected – the West Riding of Yorkshire:

> Keighley is in process of transformation from a populous, old-fashioned village, into a still more populous and flourishing town. . . . The quaint and narrow shop-windows of fifty years ago, are giving way to large panes and plate-glass. Nearly every dwelling seems devoted to some branch of commerce. . . .
>
> In a town one does not look for vivid colouring; what there may be of this is furnished by the wares in the shops, not by foliage or atmospheric effects; but in the country some brilliancy and vividness seems to be instinctively expected, and there is consequently a slight feeling of disappointment at the grey neutral tint of every object, near or far off, on the way from Keighley to Haworth. The distance is about four miles; and, as I have said, what with villas, great worsted factories, rows of workmen's houses, with here and there an old-fashioned farm-house and outbuildings, it can hardly be called 'country' any part of the way. For two miles the road passes over tolerably level ground, distant hills on the left, a 'beck' flowing through meadows on the right, and furnishing water power, at certain points, to the factories built on its banks. The air is dim and lightless with the smoke from all these

habitations and places of business. . . . Stone dykes are everywhere used in place of hedges; and what crops there are, on the patches of arable land, consist of pale, hungry-looking, grey-green oats.

Elizabeth C. Gaskell, *The Life of Charlotte Brontë* (1857), pp.1-3.

Both the drabness and the intermixing of urban and rural were early products of the 'industrial revolution', as it spread its tentacles over an ever widening area. But it must be remembered that even the largest centres, like Manchester, for long remained within walking distance of the countryside. Thus Mrs Gaskell's novel *Mary Barton* opens in a green field on a holiday afternoon, with factory workers enjoying a brief respite from their daily toil in the Manchester mills. Yet, despite the gaiety of the scene, it neatly exemplifies the chasm which was developing between the dwellers of the town and of the country in early Victorian England. The work place of the latter had become the recreation centre of the former.

There are some fields near Manchester, well known to the inhabitants as 'Green Heys Fields,' through which runs a public footpath to a little village about two miles distant. In spite of these fields being flat, and low, . . . there is a charm about them which strikes even the inhabitant of a mountainous district, who sees and feels the effect of contrast in these commonplace but thoroughly rural fields, with the busy, bustling manufacturing town he left but half-an-hour ago. Here and there an old black and white farm-house, with its rambling outbuildings, speaks of other times and other occupations than those which now absorb the population of the neighbourhood. Here in their seasons may be seen the country business of haymaking, ploughing, etc., which are such pleasant mysteries for townspeople to watch: and here the artisan, deafened with noise of tongues and engines, may come to listen awhile to the delicious sounds of rural life: the lowing of cattle, the milkmaid's call, the clatter and cackle of poultry in the old farmyards. You cannot wonder, then, that these fields are popular places of resort at every holiday time; . . . .

Elizabeth C. Gaskell, *Mary Barton* (1848), pp.1-2.

Agriculture and Marketing: The Transport Revolution

The changes in manufacturing methods were also matched by alterations in agricultural practices. Under the influence of the new trends, arable rotations were improved and a wider variety of animal fodder crops, including turnips, were grown. Although many village communities even at the end of the eighteenth century were still largely self-sufficient as regards food, the expansion of the major towns, particularly London and the industrial centres of the North, had created a market for produce which could be exploited by the bigger, more commercially minded, farmers with surpluses to sell. A measure of regional specialisation evolved, with grain production the prerogative of East Anglia and Essex, while in Kent, hop gardens, orchards and market gardens flourished alongside more traditional farming crops, and in the West country, cider was widely produced. A similar specialisation emerged among livestock farmers. Store cattle raised in Scotland, for example, were fed on Norfolk meadowland before being sent to market in London and animals bred in Brecknock and Radnor were fattened on the Essex marshes. Cheshire and parts of Wiltshire, Dorset, Suffolk and the Vale of Pickering in Yorkshire concentrated on dairy farming, while geese and capons were produced in Sussex and Surrey and turkeys and geese reached the capital from Norfolk and Suffolk.

Fairs and local markets played their part in this distribution network, often combining their economic role with a recreational one. Henry Gunning, a student at Cambridge University in the 1780s, later described the significant part played in the commercial affairs of the eastern counties by Stourbridge Fair, both for the sale of farm produce and the buying of manufactured goods:

[The] Fair was, at the time I am now speaking of [1789], a place of considerable importance, not only on account of the various trades that were carried on there, but as furnishing sights and scenes rarely to be met with out of the metropolis. ... It was the great mart at which all the dealers in cheese from Cottenham, Willingham, with other villages in the county and isle assembled; there were also traders from Leicestershire, Derbyshire, Cheshire, and Gloucestershire. Not only did the inhabitants of the neighbouring counties supply themselves with their annual stock of cheese, but great quantities were bought and sent up to London, the practice of employing travellers being at that time scarcely known. In the neighbourhood of the Chapel, ... there were about a dozen booths, called 'Ironmongers Row': these, among a great variety of other articles, furnished the goods required by saddlers and harness-makers, together with every description of leather in great abundance. ...

Another row of booths, reaching from the Chapel to Paper Mills turnpike, was called 'The Duddery'. These contained woollen cloths from Yorkshire and the western counties of England; .... There was also a very large piece of ground set apart for the sale of hops. A considerable part of the Common was occupied by earthenware and china from the Potteries, and by the coarser wares from Ely. On the left-hand side of the road, leading from the Newmarket road to the Ferry, was a row of booths extending to the Common; they consisted of silk-mercers, linendrapers, furriers, stationers, an immense variety of toys, and also of musical instruments. ... The most conspicuous person in the fair (and whose booth stood upon three times as much ground as the largest amongst them) was named Green; he came from Limehouse, and dealt in tea, sugar, soap, candles, and every other article in grocery that housekeepers could possibly require. His goods were of the first quality, and he sold them as cheap as they could be bought in London; so that any family in Cambridge, or within thirty miles of it, (who could afford the money), laid in their annual stock at that season. He was also an extensive dealer in pickles. . . .

Besides the tradesmen, there was the usual mixture of dwarfs and giants, conjurors and learned pigs. . . .

There were a great number of drinking-booths. One was on a very large scale, over the doors of which was painted, 'Quod petis hic est.' In this booth (if the weather was fine) men from the country, with their wives and families, used to feast on geese, pork, and herrings, luxuries that were to be had in great abundance, and which were served to perfection.

Henry Gunning, *Reminiscences of the University, Town, and County of Cambridge from the Year 1780* (1854), Vol. I, pp.168-72.

Much of the produce thus displayed was carried to its eventual destination by river boats or by the newly expanded canal system, while coastal shipping continued to play a major part until the mid-nineteenth century. The construction of improved turnpike roads also had its effect in opening up the countryside. And as early as 1768 the agricultural writer and improver, Arthur Young, commented upon the significance of this transport 'revolution' in increasing farmers' marketing opportunities, and hence the price they secured for their products. This applied especially to holdings located at a distance from the major markets, and there were some agriculturalists in the home counties who feared that such extra competition would undermine their own profits. But the sharp increase in the number of urban consumers showed that their fears were groundless:

London affects the price of wheat every where; and though veal and butter were very cheap in *Wales*, yet the prices of them were by no means those which arose from a home consumption alone, as I plainly perceived by the great quantities of provisions bought up in all the little ports of the *Severn*, by the *Bristol* market boats. As I drove from *Cardiff*, I met such numbers of butchers, with calves, that I inquired if that little town could consume such a quantity of veal; (it was market-day) they told me the boats were ready in the river to buy for *Bristol*. And this was doubtless the case with butter, &c. Had my private business then suffered me to penetrate further into *Wales*, beyond the course of these boats, and where no turnpike road exists, I have no doubt but I should have met with great changes in every thing, and such as would have given rise to some very important reflections. I found all the sensible people attributed the dearness of their country to the turnpike roads; and reason speaks the truth of their opinion. I can imagine many tracts of country, and there are certainly such in this kingdom, wherein provisions cannot be dear. The inhabitants of those tracts, are in the right to keep their secret; make but a turnpike-road through their country, and all the cheapness vanishes at once.

Arthur Young, *A Six Weeks' Tour Through the Southern Counties of England and Wales* (1768), pp.259-60.

Not until the 1840s and 1850s did the growth of the railway system begin to challenge the pre-eminence of these earlier forms of communication and to influence not merely the movement of goods but of people, too. Thanks to the railways, newspapers and post could also be carried around the countryside cheaply and speedily, while for the first time labouring families in rural districts remote from the coalfields were able to obtain supplies of fuel at low prices. Country shops, too, began to display the products of urban factories alongside those of purely local producers. Even such an insignificant country town as Barleyboll, in R.S. Surtees's *Mr. Sponge's Sporting Tour* (1853) could boast a fashionable London milliner, a 'merchant tailor from the same place, and a hardware shop or two, where they also sold treacle, Dartford gunpowder, pocket-handkerchiefs, sheep-nets, patent medicines, cheese, blacking, marbles, mole-traps, men's hats', among other items (p.208).

Population Increase

Accompanying these developments in manufacturing, agriculture and trading methods was a major change in the size and distribution of the population. During the years 1750 to 1800 the total number of inhabitants of England and Wales grew from an estimated six million to around nine million with the sharp upward movement continuing thereafter, at least until the 1820s. By 1851 the total population stood at about eighteen million of whom, for the first time, just over half lived in urban areas. Accompanying this, there was a steady increase in the share of people living in the industrial counties of the North. Partly this was the result of migration from other districts, but more often it was the consequence of an above average *natural* rate of increase. In 1751 perhaps 45 per cent of the population had lived in the northern or north-western counties; by 1831 that had risen to nearly 50 per cent (Phyllis Deane and W.A. Cole, *British Economic Growth 1688-1959* (1964), p.118). The share of the predominantly rural southern counties had over the same period slumped from 37.8 per cent to 31 per cent.

The reasons for this overall expansion in numbers have become the subject of much controversy over the years. Some writers have emphasised the importance of the fall in mortality rates which occurred as a result of the decline in virulence of former killer diseases like smallpox, to the effects of inoculation in preventing the latter's spread in the eighteenth century and of vaccination in reinforcing that process in the nineteenth. Other, more recent, commentators have tended to place most stress on the growth in the birth rate and the accompanying drop in the age of marriage. This has itself been attributed to the declining importance of apprenticeship in many traditional crafts and industries and to an ending of residential farm service in favour of day labour by a growing body of large capitalist farmers. Both trends removed what had formerly been barriers to early marriage and freed people to set up homes of their own. In expanding, industrialised communities, where employment opportunities were growing rapidly, these changes were particularly apparent. Even children could gain early employment and thus rapidly ceased to be a financial burden on their parents. Henry Holland in his 1808 survey of Cheshire agriculture noted that the competition for children's labour in the growing textile centres of Macclesfield, Stockport and other neighbouring towns was so keen that few boys were being brought up to farming. Consequently, it was there 'as difficult to get a boy to drive the plough, as a man to hold it'. But even in less dynamic districts, this population upsurge was apparent and, in the long run, it was to create serious problems of poverty and underemployment. The tendency for population to outstrip work opportunities in such areas inevitably weakened the workers' bargaining power and kept wages low. The pressure was further intensified by the fact that the groups who married early became proportionately more important within the village than those, like small farmers and artisans, who continued to delay marriage and child-bearing for property or apprenticeship reasons.

The effect of these trends upon one small rural community – Selborne in Hampshire – was described by the Revd Gilbert White. He had been born in the parish in 1720 and was to spend most of his life there. He wrote in the 1780s:

> The village of Selborne, and large hamlet of Oakhanger, with the single farms, and many scattered houses along the verge of the forest, contain upwards of six hundred and seventy inhabitants. . . . We abound with poor; many of whom are sober and industrious, and live comfortably in good stone or brick cottages, which are glazed, and have chambers above stairs: mud buildings we have none. Besides the employment from husbandry the men work in hop gardens, of which we have many; and fell and bark timber. In the spring and summer the women weed the corn; and enjoy a second harvest in September by hop-picking. Formerly, in the dead months they availed themselves greatly by spinning wool, for making of *barragons*, a genteel corded stuff, much in vogue at that time for summer wear; . . . but from circumstances this trade is at an end.

> The inhabitants enjoy a good share of health and longevity: and the parish swarms with children.
>
> Gilbert White, *The Natural History of Selborne*
> (1789), pp.14-16.

The process of population change and relocation was admittedly slow and as late as 1831 only about a quarter of the people lived in towns with over 20 000 inhabitants. By the end of the century that position had been transformed; then a mere quarter of the inhabitants of England and Wales still lived in rural districts.

The Advance of the Industrial Spirit and the Impact of Change

These developments, inevitably, had their social implications as a man's perception of the world often depended upon when and where he was born. Each generation accepted the practices of its own early years as standard and recorded with regret any deviations from them which it regarded as deleterious. However, for the next generation those very innovations had *themselves* become the norm and it was some fresh initiative that they feared. Hence when writers came to describe what they considered the fixed and eternal values of their childhood, what they were frequently referring to was merely a transitional phase, which had itself been praised or condemned by an earlier generation. Sydney Smith (1771-1845) was one commentator who recognised the importance of this continuing process of change, though, in his case, he welcomed the differences he discerned.

> A young man alive at this period [in the 1840s] hardly knows to what improvements of human life he has been introduced; and I would bring before his notice the changes that have taken place in England since I began to breathe the breath of life – a period of seventy years. I have been nine hours sailing from Dover to Calais before the invention of steam. It took me nine hours to go from Taunton to Bath before the invention of

railroads. In going from Taunton to Bath I suffered between ten thousand and twelve thousand severe contusions before stone-breaking MacAdam was born .... I forgot to add, that, as the basket of the stage-coaches in which luggage was then carried had no springs, your clothes were rubbed all to pieces; and that, even in the best society, one-third of the gentlemen were always drunk. I am now ashamed that I was not formerly more discontented, and am utterly surprised that all these changes and inventions did not occur two centuries ago.

> S. Baring-Gould, *Old Country Life* (1890), quoted in Frederick Watson, *Robert Smith Surtees* (1933), p.219.

But to some observers the inexorable advance of industrialisation and commercialism posed a serious threat to what they felt were the simpler verities of country life and to the social cohesiveness which the older village communities had seemed to offer. Such an approach was not new. As early as 1744 Joseph Warton had contrasted rural tranquillity with the restless and murky character of the towns of his day:

> Happy the first of men, ere yet confined
> To smoky cities; who in sheltering groves,
> Warm caves, and deep-sung valleys lived and loved
> By cares unwounded.

> Joseph Warton, *The Enthusiast: or, The Lover of Nature* (1744), ll.78-81.

Urban values he condemned as decadent and even destructive:

> O taste corrupt! that luxury and pomp
> In specious names of polished manners veiled,
> Should proudly banish Nature's simple charms.

> Ibid, ll.111-13.

With the growing pressures of industrial expansion in the second half of the eighteenth century and the burgeoning

influence of Rousseau and the Romantic movement, the
distinctions between urban and rural values became still more
clearly drawn, with the latter increasingly seen as superior,
both on moral and aesthetic grounds. William Cowper, for
example, writing in the 1780s, firmly nailed his moral colours
to the rural mast:

> God made the country, and man made the town.
> What wonder then that health and virtue, gifts
> That can alone make sweet the bitter draught
> That life holds out to all, should most abound
> And least be threaten'd in the fields and groves?
> Possess ye, therefore, ye, who, borne about
> In chariots and sedans, know no fatigue
> But that of idleness, and taste no scenes
> But such art contrives, possess ye still
> Your element; there only can ye shine,
> There only minds like your's can do no harm
>
> ⁂   ⁂   ⁂
>
> We can spare
> The splendour of your lamps; they but eclipse
> Our softer satellite. Your songs confound
> Our more harmonious notes: the thrush departs
> Scar'd, and th' offended nightingale is mute.
> There is a public mischief in your mirth;
> It plagues your country . . . .

> William Cowper, *The Task* (1785), Book I,
> ll.749-59; 764-70.

Two decades later in *The Prelude* (1805) Wordsworth
reiterated this view of the sterility of urban life, when he
compared the flurry of London with the peace of the
countryside:

> Rise up, thou monstrous ant-hill on the plain
> Of a too busy world! Before me flow,
> Thou endless stream of men and moving things!
>
> ⁂   ⁂   ⁂

the deafening din;
The comers and the goers face to face,
Face after face; the string of dazzling wares,
Shop after shop, with symbols, blazoned names,
And all the tradesman's honours overhead:

✻   ✻   ✻

Meanwhile the roar continues, till at length,
Escaped as from an enemy, we turn
Abruptly into some sequestered nook,
Still as a sheltered place when winds blow loud!

William Wordsworth, *The Prelude* (1850 text),
Book VII, ll.149-51; 155-59; 168-71.

As Roger Sales has pointed out, such a vision of pastoral serenity conveniently ignored the harsher realities of day-to-day life on the land. It gave no indication of the long hours of drudging labour expected from most peasant cultivators or the feudal dues exacted from them by many landowners in Wordsworth's native Cumbria (*English Literature in History: Pastoral and Politics 1780-1830* (1983), p.58). This is rather a 'countryside of the mind' – a place of intellectual refuge – than one rooted in the reality of Georgian England.

Nevertheless, the belief that these rural ideals were under threat from an expanding commercialism was immensely strengthened in the late eighteenth century. As a modern critic, W.J. Keith, has somewhat sardonically observed: 'it is no coincidence that the romantic cult of wild nature flourished just at the time when the Industrial Revolution was gaining momentum; the countryside is cherished only when it is seriously threatened – and it is cherished most by those who threaten it'. (*The Rural Tradition* (1975), p.11).

But Keith's comments also bring out another point – namely, that because many writers on country life depended upon urban readers for the sale of their books, this possibly influenced the character of their work. It may have called forth a nostalgic portrayal of an idealised rural scene, divorced from stern reality, because this was the viewpoint that the townsman, in search of relaxation and escapism, wished to receive. That aspect was recognised by Robert Bloomfield, the Suffolk labourer turned shoemaker and poet, whose immensely successful *The Farmer's Boy* (1800) sold 26 000 copies within three years of publication. In 1814, when writing to a friend about his current financial difficulties, he added half-mockingly:

> I sometimes dream that I shall one day venture again before the public something [in] my old manner; some Country tales, and spiced with love and courtship might yet please, for Rural life by the art of Cookery may be made a relishing and high flavoured dish, whatever it may be in reality . . . .
>
> British Library, Add. MSS 28, 268; f.351.

John Britton, the self-educated nineteenth-century topographer, who started life working on the land, similarly emphasised the way in which much writing on rural affairs was divorced from the unpalatable truth:

> Many poets and essayists have eulogized rustic life and manners, as being replete with sylvan joys, arcadian scenes, primeval innocence, and unsophisticated pleasures. Alas! these are but the closet dreams of metropolitan poets and visionary enthusiasts; for I fear that all their pleasing pictures are wholly drawn from imagination, and not from nature. The genuine rustics, I believe, in all counties, and I apprehend in all nations, have very little more sagacity than the animals with whom they associate, and of whose natures they partake: . . . .
>
> *The Autobiography of John Britton*, Part I (1850), p.59.

Contemporary Views

In accepting the veracity of contemporary accounts of the rural scene, therefore, we must take into the reckoning the writers' own hidden motives and prejudices. The need to please a patron, to confound an enemy, or, as in the case of the Victorian novelist and statesman, Benjamin Disraeli, to promote a political philosophy, could all play their part in influencing the final text. Differences in perception likewise occurred as a consequence of the personalities of the authors. Thus Oliver Goldsmith, in the 1760s, became concerned at the widening gap between rich and poor, and the way in which some small peasant farmers were being deprived of their livelihood and independence by the selfish actions of wealthy individuals concerned to build up large estates or surround their mansions with landscaped parks:

> Ye friends to truth, ye statesmen who survey
> The rich man's joy increase, the poor's decay,
> 'Tis yours to judge, how wide the limits stand
> Between a splendid and an happy land.

✳   ✳   ✳

> The man of wealth and pride
> Takes up a space that many poor supplied;
> Space for his lake, his park's extended bounds,
> Space for his horses, equipage, and hounds:
> The robe that wraps his limbs in silken sloth
> Has robbed the neighbouring fields of half their
>   growth;
> His seat, where solitary sports are seen,
> Indignant spurns the cottage from the green: . . . .

Oliver Goldsmith, The Deserted Village (1770),
ll.265-68; 275-82.

It was a situation which he contrasted sharply with the peace and security of the 'old' village life, as depicted both in the opening lines of this poem, and in his *Vicar of Wakefield* (1766) (See Chapter 2, pp.29-30). But as early as June 1762 he had written anonymously in *Lloyd's Evening Post* to describe events which he had himself witnessed, and which had fuelled his disquiet:

I spent part of the last summer in a little village, distant
about fifty miles from town, consisting of near an
hundred houses. It lay entirely out of the road of
commerce, and was inhabited by a race of men who
followed the primeval profession of agriculture for
several generations. Though strangers to opulence, they
were unacquainted with distress; few of them were
known either to acquire a fortune or to die in indigence.
By a long intercourse and frequent intermarriages they
were all become in a manner one family; and, when the
work of the day was done, spent the night agreeably in
visits at each other's houses. Upon those occasions the
poor traveller and stranger were always welcome; and
they kept up the stated days of festivity with the
strictest observance. They were merry at Christmas and
mournful in Lent, got drunk on St. George's-day, and
religiously cracked nuts on Michaelmas-eve.

Upon my first arrival I felt a secret pleasure in
observing this happy community. The chearfulness of
the old, and the blooming beauty of the young, was no
disagreeable change to one like me, whose whole life
had been spent in cities. But my satisfaction was soon
repressed, when I understood that they were shortly to
leave this abode of felicity, of which they and their
ancestors had been in possession time immemorial, and
that they had received orders to seek for a new
habitation. I was informed that a Merchant of immense
fortune in London, who had lately purchased the estate
on which they lived, intended to lay the whole out in a
seat of pleasure for himself. I staid 'till the day on which
they were compelled to remove, and own I never felt so
sincere a concern before.

I was grieved to see a generous, virtuous race of men,
who should be considered as the strength and the
ornament of their country, torn from their little
habitations, and driven out to meet poverty and
hardship among strangers. No longer to earn and enjoy
the fruits of their labour, they were now going to toil as
hirelings under some rigid Master, to flatter the opulent
for a precarious meal, and to leave their children the

inheritance of want and slavery. . . . All the connexions of kindred were now irreparably broken; their neat gardens and well cultivated fields were left to desolation. . . .

Such was their misery, and I could wish that this were the only instance of such migrations of late. But I am informed that nothing is at present more common than such revolutions. In almost every part of the kingdom the laborious husbandman has been reduced, and the lands are now either occupied by some general undertaker, or turned into enclosures destined for the purposes of amusement or luxury. Wherever the traveller turns, while he sees one part of the inhabitants of the country becoming immensely rich, he sees the other growing miserably poor, and the happy equality of condition now entirely removed. . . .

A country, thus parcelled out among the rich alone, is of all others the most miserable. The Great, in themselves, perhaps, are not so bad as they are generally represented; but I have almost ever found the dependents and favourites of the Great, strangers to every sentiment of honour and generosity. Wretches, who, by giving up their own dignity to those above them, insolently exact the same tribute from those below.

> *Lloyd's Evening Post*, 14-16 June 1762. (Attributed to Oliver Goldsmith in Vol. III of *Collected Works of Oliver Goldsmith*, ed. A. Friedman.)

This ominous vision of a countryside under threat as a result of the exercise of individual power, wealth and commercial instincts was, however, firmly rejected by the cooler pen of Sir Frederic M. Eden, writing less than four decades later, but from a very different standpoint. 'Deserted villages in Great Britain', he firmly declared, 'now are only to be found in the fictions of poetry. Our agricultural parishes are better stocked now than they were one hundred years ago when industry had not purged the country of its superfluous mouths and the visionary evils ascribed to the existence of commercial and agricultural capitalists did not exist.' (Sir Frederic M. Eden, *An Estimate of the Number of Inhabitants of Great Britain and Ireland* (1800), pp.48-49.) Part of the change was due to the different economic circumstances of the country, then in the midst of its long war with revolutionary France, as compared to Goldsmith's time, but part was also due to the difference of perception between the two writers.

Goldsmith's picture of a village in danger of social fragmentation as a result of hostile external forces being brought to bear upon it likewise differed radically from the view put forward by Mary Russell Mitford in the early 1820s. She was writing from the Berkshire hamlet of Three Mile Cross, where she had made her home, and to her it was the sense of community and security of village life which was most important. After the ending of the Napoleonic Wars in 1815 agriculture became seriously depressed and there was much misery and unemployment within the countryside. But those aspects were virtually ignored by Miss Mitford. The opening lines of the first volume of *Our Village* (serialised in 1822 and published in book form two years later) made clear what she found so attractive about the rural world:

Of all situations for a constant residence, that which appears to me most delightful is a little village far in the country; a small neighbourhood, not of fine mansions finely peopled, but of cottages and cottage-like houses, . . . with inhabitants whose faces are as familiar to us as the flowers in our garden; a little world of our own, close-packed and insulated like ants in an ant-hill, or bees in a hive, or sheep in a fold, . . .; where we know every one, are known to every one, interested in every one, and authorized to hope that every one feels an interest in us. How pleasant it is to slide into these true-hearted feelings from the kindly and unconscious influence of habit, and to learn to know and to love the people about us, with all their peculiarities, just as we learn to know and to love the nooks and turns of the shady lanes and sunny commons that we pass every day. Even in books I like a confined locality . . . . Nothing is so tiresome as to be whirled half over

Europe at the chariot-wheels of a hero, to go to sleep at Vienna, and awaken at Madrid; it produces a real fatigue, a weariness of spirit. On the other hand, nothing is so delightful as to sit down in a country village in one of Miss Austen's delicious novels, quite sure before we leave it to become intimate with every spot and every person it contains; or to ramble with Mr. White over his own parish of Selborne, and form a friendship with the fields and coppices, as well as with the birds, mice, and squirrels, who inhabit them; . . . . And a small neighbourhood is as good in sober waking reality as in poetry or prose; a village neighbourhood, such as this Berkshire hamlet in which I write, a long, straggling, winding street at the bottom of a fine eminence, with a road through it, always abounding in carts, horsemen, and carriages, and lately enlivened by a stage-coach. . . . Will you walk with me through our village, courteous reader?

Mary Russell Mitford, *Our Village* Vol. I (1824),
pp.1-3.

And the reader accepts that invitation, secure in the knowledge that his sensibilities will not be offended by the squalid or the miserable, and that it is only with the happy and peaceful side of country life that he will be confronted.

By contrast, that pugnacious critic of the growing power of the commercial interest and of the effects of agricultural recession, William Cobbett, portrayed a very different rural scene. Like Miss Mitford, he was writing in the 1820s. Indeed, his family and hers had once been close friends. But his perceptions were far removed from the serenity she offered. Not only did he castigate the pretensions of the larger farmers, who had prospered in the era of high food prices during the Napoleonic Wars, but, unlike Mary Mitford, he bemoaned the passing of a village 'golden age' recollected from his youth. His very different view of the late Georgian countryside is exemplified in the following extract, written at Reigate, Surrey, on 20 October 1825.

Having done my business at Hartswood to-day
about eleven o'clock, I went to a sale at a farm, which
the farmer is quitting. Here I had a view of what has
long been going on all over the country. . . .
Everything about this farm-house was formerly the
scene of *plain manners* and *plentiful living*. Oak
clothes-chests, oak bedsteads, oak chests of drawers,
and oak tables to eat on, long, strong, and well supplied
with joint stools. Some of the things were many
hundreds of years old. But all appeared to be in a state of
decay and nearly of *disuse*. There appeared to have been
hardly any *family* in that house, where formerly there
were, in all probability, from ten to fifteen men, boys,
and maids: and, which was the worst of all, there was a
parlour. Aye, and a *carpet* and *bell-pull* too! One end of
the front of this once plain and substantial house had
been moulded into a *"parlour;"* and there was the
mahogany table, and the fine chairs, and the fine glass,
and all as bare-faced upstart as any stock-jobber in the
kingdom can boast of. And there were the decanters,
the glasses, the "dinner-set" of crockery-ware, and all
just in the true stock-jobber style. And I dare say it has
been *'Squire* Charington and the *Miss* Charington's;
and not plain Master Charington, and his son Hodge,
and his daughter Betty Charington, all of whom this
accursed system has, in all likelihood, transmuted into a
species of mock gentlefolks, while it has ground the
labourers down into real slaves. Why do not farmers
now *feed* and *lodge* their work-people, as they did
formerly? Because they cannot keep them *upon so little*
as they give them in wages. This is the real cause of the
change. There needs no more to prove that the lot of the
working classes has become worse than it formerly was.
This fact alone is quite sufficient to settle this point. All
the world knows that a number of people, boarded in
the same house, and at the same table, can, with as good
food, be boarded much cheaper than those persons
divided into twos, threes, or fours, can be boarded. This
is a well-known truth: therefore, if the farmer now
shuts his pantry against his labourers, and pays them
wholly in money, is it not clear that he does it because

he thereby gives them a living *cheaper* to him; that is to say, a *worse* living than formerly? Mind, he has a *house* for them; a kitchen for them to sit in, bedrooms for them to sleep in, tables, and stools, and benches, of ever-lasting duration. All these he has: . . . and yet so much does he gain by pinching them in wages that he lets all these things remain as of no use rather than feed labourers in the house. Judge, then, of the *change* that has taken place in the condition of these labourers! And be astonished, if you can, at the *pauperism* and the *crimes* that now disgrace this once happy and moral England.

The land produces, on an average, what it always produced, but there is a new distribution of the produce. This 'Squire Charington's father used, I dare say, to sit at the head of the oak-table along with his men, say grace to them, and cut up the meat and the pudding. He might take a cup of *strong beer* to himself, when they had none; but that was pretty nearly all the difference in their manner of living. So that *all* lived well. But the *'squire* had many *wine-decanters* and *wine-glasses* and *"a dinner set,"* and a *"breakfast set,"* and *"dessert knives;"* and these evidently imply carryings on and a consumption that must of necessity have greatly robbed the long oak table if it had remained fully tenanted. That long table could not share in the work of the decanters and the dinner set. Therefore, it became almost untenanted; the labourers retreated to hovels, called cottages; and instead of board and lodging, they got money; so little of it as to enable the employer to drink wine; but, then, that he might not reduce them to *quite starvation*, they were enabled to come to him, in the *king's name*, and demand food *as paupers.*

William Cobbett, *Rural Rides* (1825), Vol. I, pp.265-67.

Mary Mitford and William Cobbett, each in their own way, portrayed what they saw as the truth of contemporary country life, but clearly their respective understandings of that reality had little in common. For Cobbett it was the harshness of the current social scene which came through most clearly, not the strength of communal ties, whereas for Mary Mitford the reverse was the case. A third variation on the theme was provided by George Borrow, whose travels through England in the 1820s and beyond were very much concerned with the less 'respectable' side of life. It is his encounters with gypsies, tinkers, pedlars, boxers and other 'fringe' characters that principally interest him. Not only did he learn the Romany language, but he became fast friends with the Romany leader, Jasper Petulengro. This did not blind him to the gypsies' faults – their willingness to poison a farmer's pigs or to pass forged coinage, but it gave him great sympathy with their way of life, which he occasionally shared:

> I had frequent interviews with Jasper, sometimes in his tent, sometimes on the heath, about which we would roam for hours, discoursing on various matters. Sometimes mounted on one of his horses, of which he had several, I would accompany him to various fairs and markets in the neighbourhood, to which he went on his own affairs, or those of his tribe. I soon found that I had become acquainted with a most singular people, whose habits and pursuits awakened within me the highest interest. Of all connected with them, however, their language was doubtless that which exercised the greatest influence over my imagination . . . this strange broken tongue, spoken by people who dwelt among thickets and furze bushes in tents as tawny as their faces, and whom the generality of mankind designated, and with much semblance of justice, as thieves and vagabonds. But where did this speech come from, and who were they who spoke it? These were questions which I could not solve, and which Jasper himself, when pressed, confessed his inability to answer. 'But, whoever we be, brother,' said he, 'we are an old people, and not what folks in general imagine, broken gorgios; and, if we are not Egyptians, we are at any rate Rommany Chals!'

George Borrow, *Lavengro* (1851), pp.114-15.

Perhaps the severest critic of the comfortable pastoral image of the countryside presented by some contemporary commentators was George Eliot. As the daughter of a Warwickshire land agent and farmer, she had witnessed at first hand the daily round of rural life and was fiercely critical of those writers and painters who sought to present the village as a happy playground of contented shepherds and farmers, experiencing with their wives and families an existence of sylvan innocence. George Eliot was born in November 1819 at South Farm, Arbury, and continued to reside in her native county until her father's death in 1849:

> The notion that peasants are joyous, that the typical moment to represent a man in a smock-frock is when he is cracking a joke and showing a row of sound teeth, that cottage matrons are usually buxom, and village children necessarily rosy and merry, are prejudices difficult to dislodge from the artistic mind, which looks for its subjects into literature instead of life. The painter is still under the influence of idyllic literature, which has always expressed the imagination of the cultivated and town-bred, rather than the truth of rustic life. Idyllic ploughmen are jocund when they drive their team afield; idyllic shepherds make bashful love under hawthorn-bushes; idyllic villagers dance in the chequered shade and refresh themselves, not immoderately, with spicy nut-brown ale. But no one who has seen much of actual ploughmen thinks them jocund; no one who is well acquainted with the English peasantry can pronounce them merry. The slow gaze, in which no sense of beauty beams, no humour twinkles, – the slow utterance, and the heavy slouching walk, remind one rather of that melancholy animal the camel, than of the sturdy countryman, with striped stockings, red waistcoat, and hat aside, who represents the traditional English peasant. Observe a company of haymakers. When you see them at a distance, tossing up the forkfuls of hay in the golden light, while the waggon creeps slowly with its increasing burthen over the meadow, and the bright green space which tells of work

done gets larger and larger, you pronounce the scene 'smiling', and you think these companions in labour must be as bright and cheerful as the picture to which they give animation. Approach nearer, and you will certainly find that haymaking-time is a time for joking, especially if there are women among the labourers; but the coarse laugh that bursts out every now and then, and expresses the triumphant taunt, is as far as possible from your conception of idyllic merriment. That delicious effervescence of the mind which we call fun, has no equivalent for the northern peasant, except tipsy revelry; the only realm of fancy and imagination for the English clown exists at the bottom of the third quart-pot.

The conventional countryman of the stage, who picks up pocket-books and never looks into them, and who is too simple even to know that honesty has its opposite, represents the still lingering mistake, that an unintelligible dialect is a guarantee for ingenuousness, and that slouching shoulders indicate an upright disposition. It is quite true that a thresher is likely to be innocent of any adroit arithmetical cheating, but he is not the less likely to carry home his master's corn in his shoes and pocket; a reaper is not given to writing begging-letters, but he is quite capable of cajoling the dairymaid into filling his small-beer bottle with ale. The selfish instincts are not subdued by the sight of buttercups, nor is integrity in the least established by that classic rural occupation, sheep-washing. To make men moral, something more is requisite than to turn them out to grass . . . .

George Eliot, 'English Peasants' in *Westminster Review, New Series*, Vol. X, 1 July 1856, pp.53-54.

It has been the aim of this chapter to focus upon some of the major themes of rural life which will be explored in the following chapters, and to warn the reader of the differing, even contradictory, interpretations placed upon those issues by contemporary commentators. True objectivity is a rare quality, and writers, like other men and women, are influenced by personal prejudice and individual inclination. The differing approach of Mary Russell Mitford and William Cobbett was reflected in the contributions of many other observers of the rural scene between 1760 and the 1850s. Certainly the romantic, pastoral view of a world of natural innocence threatened by the corrosive values of urban society, which informs much of Wordsworth's work, bears little resemblance to the pessimistic, censorious picture of Georgian village life portrayed by the Suffolk-born poet, George Crabbe. Equally, writers are affected by the 'spirit of the age', and such mid-century novels as *Yeast* and *Alton Locke*, produced by the country cleric and Christian Socialist, Charles Kingsley, clearly mirrored the growing concern for the plight of the poor which began to manifest itself in the 1840s and 1850s.

Finally, in this survey of Georgian and early Victorian country life use has been made both of factual material and literary sources, including novels. For as a recent critic has shrewdly observed: 'In other languages than English the same word serves for both "history" and "story", emphasizing the close relations between historical and fictional narratives. Novels can provide historical knowledge, and even be a form of history; while historiography uses many of the devices of the novel.' (Bernard Bergonzi, *Times Higher Educational Supplement*, 11 January 1985, p.17.)

2 Village Life and Labour, 1760-1815

Landed property was the foundation of eighteenth-century society. The soil itself yielded the nation its sustenance and most of its raw materials, and provided the population with its most extensive means of employment; and the owners of the soil derived from its consequence and wealth the right to govern. . . . The wealth, power and social influence produced by ownership of land enabled the landowning classes to control all local government beyond the bounds of the larger towns and to secure a dominating representation in Parliament itself.

G.E. Mingay, *English Landed Society in the Eighteenth Century* (1963), p.3.

Landownership and Village Society

Already by the middle of the eighteenth century a tripartite system of land cultivation – comprising landlord, tenant farmer, and wage labourer – had become established over most of England. At the end of the century more than three-quarters of all the cultivated land was tilled by tenants, many of whom employed labourers. Only in Wales and a few English counties, such as parts of Lancashire, Cheshire and North Yorkshire, with their dairying preoccupations, or Cumbria, with its sheep-farming enterprises, was society composed of owner-occupiers or landlords and small rent-paying family producers. The homely surroundings of many of these minor proprietors was described by Emily Brontë in the opening pages of *Wuthering Heights*. Although first published in 1847, the book was set in the Yorkshire of the early nineteenth century:

One step brought us into the family sitting-room, without any introductory lobby, or passage: they call it here 'the house' pre-eminently. It includes kitchen, and parlour, generally, but I believe at Wuthering Heights the kitchen is forced to retreat altogether into another quarter, at least I distinguished a chatter of tongues, and a clatter of culinary utensils, deep within; . . . . One end, indeed, reflected splendidly both light and heat, from ranks of immense pewter dishes, interspersed with silver jugs and tankards, towering row after row, in a vast oak dresser, to the very roof. The latter had never been underdrawn, its entire anatomy laid bare to an inquiring eye, except where a frame of wood laden with oatcakes, and clusters of legs of beef, mutton, and ham, concealed it. Above the chimney were sundry villainous old guns, and a couple of horse-pistols, and, by way of ornament, three gaudily painted canisters disposed along its ledge. The floor was of smooth, white stone: the chairs, high-backed, primitive structures, painted green: one or two heavy black ones lurking in the shade. . . .

The apartment and furniture would have been nothing extraordinary as belonging to a . . . northern farmer with a stubborn countenance, and stalwart limbs, set out to advantage in knee-breeches, and gaiters. Such an individual, seated in his armchair, his mug of ale frothing on the round table before him, is to be seen in any circuit of five or six miles among these hills, if you go at the right time, after dinner.

Emily Brontë, *Wuthering Heights* (1847), pp.46-47.

Alongside the farmers and agricultural labourers were the village tradesmen, who ministered to their wants by the exercise of a wide variety of skills. Foremost among them were the blacksmiths, who made and repaired farm implements as well as the cooking pans of householders and the gardening tools of labourers. They also shod the horses which were the principal draught animals for all kinds of haulage work. Then there were the builders and carpenters who maintained the dwellings and the furniture of their fellow parishioners. They included men like Adam and Seth Bede, who painstakingly practised their skills, alongside three fellow craftsmen, in the small workshop of Mr Jonathan Burge of Hayslope. There they busied themselves

> upon doors and window-frames and wainscoting. A scent of pine-wood from a tent-like pile of planks outside the open door mingled itself with the scent of the elderbushes . . .; the slanting sunbeams shone through the transparent shavings that flew before the steady plane, and lit up the fine grain of the oak panelling which stood propped against the wall. On a heap of those soft shavings a rough grey shepherd-dog had made himself a pleasant bed, and was lying with his nose between his fore-paws, occasionally wrinkling his brows to cast a glance at the tallest of the five workmen, who was carving a shield in the centre of a wooden mantelpiece. It was to this workman that the strong baritone belonged which was heard above the sound of plane and hammer singing . . . .

> George Eliot, *Adam Bede* (1859), p.7.

Tailors and dressmakers were responsible for making the clothes that people wore, while shoemakers produced boots and leggings.

Often a farmer would pay for these services in kind rather than cash, perhaps by providing corn or other farm produce, or by free carriage of winter fuel and the supply of a ley for the craftsman's livestock. 'In winter when cultivation was at a standstill, the farmers would use their idle [horse] teams in fetching wood or coal, the roads permitting, not only for themselves but also for the squire, parson and other neighbours who had no wagons of their own'. (G.E. Mingay, *English Landed Society in the Eighteenth Century* (1963), p.239.) However, in many southern counties, where fuel was scarce and dear, poorer people were unable to afford their own fires, even for cooking, and had to share with a neighbour. The misery that caused during the cold winter months is easy to imagine.

Within this carefully regulated environment each person knew his or her place and would normally expect to remain in it. Emma Woodhouse, the eponymous heroine of Jane Austen's novel (1815), whose family was 'first in consequence' in the village of Highbury, made clear the distinctions when she firmly informed her friend, Harriet Smith, that

> A young farmer, whether on horseback or on foot, is the very last sort of person to raise my curiosity. The yeomanry are precisely the order of people with whom I feel I can have nothing to do. A degree or two lower, and a creditable appearance might interest me; I might hope to be useful to their families in some way or other. But a farmer can need none of my help, and is therefore in one sense as much above my notice as in every other he is below it.
>
> Jane Austen, *Emma* (1815), p.25.

She then went on to dismiss Harriet's admirer, the substantial tenant farmer, Robert Martin, as

> very plain, undoubtedly – remarkably plain: – but that is nothing, compared with his entire want of gentility. I had no right to expect much, and I did not expect much; but I had no idea that he could be so very clownish, so totally without air. I had imagined him, I confess, a degree or two nearer gentility.
>
> Ibid, p.28.

In an ideal world these social divisions were accepted by the inhabitants without rancour, in a spirit of neighbourliness. It was such a picture of communal content that Goldsmith presented in *The Vicar of Wakefield*, with most of the rough edges of economic reality carefully smoothed away:

> The place of our retreat was in a little neighbourhood, consisting of farmers, who tilled their own grounds, and were equal strangers to opulence and poverty. As they had almost all the conveniences of life within themselves, they seldom visited towns or cities in search

of superfluity. Remote from the polite, they still retained the primaeval simplicity of manners, and frugal by habit, they scarce knew that temperance was a virtue. They wrought with chearfulness on days of labour; but observed festivals as intervals of idleness and pleasure. They kept up the Christmas carol, sent true love-knots on Valentine morning, eat pancakes on Shrove-tide, shewed their wit on the first of April, and religiously cracked nuts on Michaelmas eve. Being apprized of our approach, the whole neighbourhood came out to meet their minister, drest in their finest cloaths, and preceded by a pipe and tabor: A feast also was provided for our reception, at which we sat chearfully down; and what the conversation wanted in wit, was made up in laughter. ... My farm consisted of about twenty acres of excellent land, having given an hundred pound for my predecessor's good-will. ...

As we rose with the sun, so we never pursued our labours after it was gone down, but returned home to the expecting family; where smiling looks, a neat hearth, and pleasant fire, were prepared for our reception. Nor were we without guests: sometimes farmer Flamborough, our talkative neighbour, and often the blind piper, would pay us a visit, and taste our gooseberry wine; for the making of which we had lost neither the receipt nor the reputation. These harmless people had several ways of being good company, while one played, the other would sing some soothing ballad. ... The night was concluded in the manner we began the morning, my youngest boys being appointed to read the lessons of the day, and he that read loudest, distinctest, and best, was to have an halfpenny on Sunday to put into the poor's box.

Oliver Goldsmith, *The Vicar of Wakefield* (1766),
in Arthur Friedman, *Collected Works of Oliver
Goldsmith* (1966) Vol. IV, pp.31-33.

At the summit of this social system were the major landlords, men with estates of five thousand acres or more, enjoying an annual income of at least five or six thousand pounds. At the end of the eighteenth century perhaps four hundred families fell into this category, owning between them around 20 to 25 per cent of the cultivated land of England. Among them were a few men of exceptional wealth, like the Dukes of Bedford, Devonshire and Northumberland, or the Earl of Egremont, whose incomes might approach £40 000 or £50 000 a year, more than was enjoyed by many small independent rulers on the continent. Their luxurious lifestyle, retinues of servants, and wide political influence distinguished them from the lesser ranks of landed society and enabled them to support both a large country mansion and the expenses of a London season. A number, indeed, preferred to spend their time away from their estates, savouring the pleasures of the gaming table, the theatre and the racecourse or undertaking a grand tour of Europe, whilst their households were left in the care of the servants. Racing was particularly popular, with the subscription list of the *Racing Calendar* for 1768, for example, headed by nine dukes and nineteen earls, as well as lesser nobility and gentry. Many also owned more than one estate; in 1779 the Duke of Bolton had no fewer than six seats in five counties. Inevitably some of the secondary houses became enormous white elephants, little or never lived in, and either rented out to tenants or allowed to go to rack and ruin for want of attention.

The hospitality of these grandees was normally as lavish as their own mode of life. Thus the French traveller, B. Faujas Saint-Fond, who visited Britain in 1784, subsequently described an agreeable interlude spent with the Duke of Argyll at Inverary castle:

> Each person rose at any hour he pleased in the mornng. Some took a ride, others went to the chace. I rose with the sun, and proceeded to examine the natural history of the environs.
>
> At ten o'clock, a bell summoned us to breakfast: we then repaired to a large room, ornamented with historical pictures of the Argyle (*sic*) family. . . . Here we found several breakfast tables, covered with tea, coffee, excellent cream, and every thing the appetite

could desire, surrounded with bouquets of flowers, newspapers, and books. There were, besides, in this room, a billiard-table, a piano-forte, and other musical instruments.

After breakfast, some walked in the parks, others amused themselves with reading and music, or returned to their apartments. At half past four, the dinner bell was rung, and we went to the dining-room, where we always found a table of twenty-five or thirty covers. When all the company were seated, the chaplain, according to custom, made a short prayer, and blest the food, which was eat with pleasure. . . . The different courses, and the aftermeats, were all done as in France, and with the same variety and abundance. If the poultry were not so juicy as that of Paris, we were amply compensated by the most delicate moorfowl, by delicious fish, and by vegetables, the quality of which did honour to the skill of the Scottish gardeners.

At the dessert, the scene changed; cloth, napkins, and every thing disappeared. The mahogany table shone in all the lustre that wood is capable of receiving from art; but it was soon covered with brilliant decanters, filled with the most exquisite wines; comfits, in fine porcelain, or crystal, vases; and fruits of different kinds in beautiful baskets. Plates and glasses were distributed; and in every object elegance and conveniency seemed to rival each other . . . .

Towards the end of the dessert, the ladies withdrew to a room destined for the tea-table: I was sorry that they left us so long alone; but the Duke of Argyle informed me, that he preserved this old custom in his family, in order that the people of the country might not be offended by the breach of a practice, to which they had always been accustomed. The ceremony of toasts was well kept up in the absence of the ladies; but though they usually continued to go round for at least three quarters of an hour no person's inclination was violated, and every one drank what he pleased. . . .

At last they proceeded to the drawing-room, where tea and coffee abound, and where the ladies did the honours of the table with much dignity and grace . . . .

After tea, those who chused it retired to their apartments; those who preferred conversation and music remained in the room; others went out to walk. At ten o'clock supper was ready, and those attended it who pleased.

B. Faujas Saint-Fond, *Travels in England, Scotland and the Hebrides* (1799), Vol. 1, pp.251-58.

Below these major landowners came the gentry, who shared many of their interests and prejudices, and were chiefly distinguished from them by their lower incomes. They ranged from men with £3000 to £4000 a year down to a very large body of perhaps ten to twenty thousand families who could muster no more than £300 to £1000 a year. As a group the wealthy gentry, smaller squires and country gentlemen owned around 50 to 60 per cent of the cultivated land in the late eighteenth century. Although most were from long-established county families, they were joined throughout the period by a steady inflow of 'new' men – merchants, lawyers, and even a few industrialists – who sought the status which landed property could bestow. The counties around London were dotted with the country seats of lawyers and merchants from the capital, while in the north of England, too, a similar trend emerged. Liverpool merchants appeared as lords of the manor as far afield as Westmorland. Inevitably, at least in the early stages, they remained on the fringes of true 'landed' society, although their sons and grandsons could hope for a gradual assimilation into that charmed circle.

But significant though family background was, income remained an important criterion in deciding just where a man stood in the social pecking order. It is notable that Jane Austen frequently used the fortunes of the families she was describing as a way of indicating their position in the world. Mr Rushworth in *Mansfield Park*, with £12 000 a year, was the richest of her characters, though Mr Darcy in *Pride and Prejudice*, with £10 000, could boast a park ten miles in circumference, as well as a large, handsome stone mansion elegantly built on rising ground, and a property in London. On a humbler level was Henry Crawford, also in *Mansfield Park*, who could boast no more than £4000 a year.

On the other hand, none save the wealthiest tenant farmers could aspire to the financial position of even the poorest members of the gentry. Their average incomes probably ranged between £100 and £300 a year only. Yet, during the era of high food prices in the 1790s and early 1800s some of the larger and more prosperous farmers strove to attain the living standards of the humbler country gentlemen. Cartoonists like Gillray savagely mocked the pretensions of men who were too proud to eat with their labourers, kept a piano in their drawing room and sent their daughters to boarding school. Even the Norfolk parson, James Woodforde, commented on the changing times in August 1796: 'Mrs. Howlett was at Church and exhibited for the first time, a black Vail over her Face. Mem. Times must be good for Farmers when their Wives can dress in such stile'. (James Woodforde, *The Diary of a Country Parson 1758-1802*, p.531.)

For agricultural labourers, by contrast, annual income even in the 1790s could be as little as the £9 or £10 paid to men living in as farm servants – carters, milkers, and the like – and rising to perhaps £20 to £40 for those with their own cottages. In the period of war-time inflation, these low earnings fell still further behind the rise in prices. Overall, the cash wages of farm workers increased by perhaps 75 per cent at a time when prices had more than doubled. Small wonder that in the famine year of 1801 Arthur Young could remark that 'the quantity of food which a labourer could once have bought for 5s. would now cost him 26s. 6d., supposing he had the money to pay for it'. Most workers had not. (See J.D. Chambers and G.E. Mingay, *The Agricultural Revolution 1750-1880* (1966), p.119.)

Meanwhile, for the landowner, his income from property bestowed a prestige and authority which no other form of wealth could command. It also gave him the ability, as a magistrate, to run local government, as well as to play a dominating role within parliament. Perhaps two-thirds of the members of the House of Commons in the eighteenth century were landowners and a high proportion of the hundred or so members whose profession was in trade or the armed services had family ties with the aristocracy.

Along with this power, at least in theory, went certain clearly defined responsibilities. Although there were rogues and spendthrifts within their ranks, most landowners understood they had a duty towards those under their jurisdiction. Often this meant sacrificing the pleasures of London society or the amenities offered by inland spas such as Bath, Tunbridge Wells and Cheltenham or seaside resorts like Brighton and Scarborough to spend time in the country upon their estates. Joseph Farington, who visited Chatsworth in 1801, noted approvingly that the Duke and Duchess of Devonshire had spent the previous winter in Derbyshire. 'The advantages of their residing here were felt essentially by the neighboroud (*sic*). The Duke was in a great stile, having sometimes in His House 180 persons, including Visitors & their servants. He kills on an average 5 bullocks in a fortnight and 15 or 16 sheep a week. The Horses of the Visitors are recd. in His Stables so long as they will hold them the rest are sent to the Inn. . . . Many pensions of £5 a year are allowed to poor people in this village & in the neighboroud by His grace whose goodness is extensively felt'. (Joseph Farington, *The Farington Diary* (1922), Vol. I, p.313.)

It also became customary for landlords to entertain tenants, labourers, and schoolchildren to dinners, dances and other junketings, perhaps to celebrate the coming-of-age or the birthday of a member of the family. At Stowe Lady Buckingham's birthday was regularly celebrated by a dance and supper for the farmers, followed by a supper for three hundred poor people on the following evening. And her son's birthday, a few days later, was marked by a supper for poor children and a servants' ball. In December 1804 one lady visitor described her attendance at Lady Buckingham's birthday dance for the tenants with less than enthusiasm. 'In the evening we all danced with the tenants. . . . I laughed a great deal to see the different mixture of people. We could hardly breathe it was so hot and the smell was beyond anything. We danced Sir Roger de Coverly (*sic*), attended their supper &c. Delighted were we to go to bed.' (Anne Fremantle, ed., *The Wynne Diaries 1789-1820*, p.373.) But for the landed families involved it was an important way of cementing personal relationships with the local people.

Inevitably in an age when agricultural improvement loomed large in the consciousness of many leading landowners from the King (George III) downwards, there was interest in the practical running of estates and the organisation of model farms. The fact that, in the long run, these developments often led to higher rentals also increased their attractiveness. But landowners frequently acquired the best livestock or the newest farm implements for prestige reasons rather than purely economic ones, rather as they desired to own fast horses or a pack of foxhounds. The famous paintings by George Stubbs of favourite horses, hounds and hunting scenes were commissioned for much the same reason.

Nevertheless, there was a more serious motive at work, too. As the agricultural improver, Nathaniel Kent, declared in a letter to his patron, George III, when putting forward proposals for a reorganisation of the Great Park at Windsor, '*Agriculture* is unquestionably, one of the most rational, and laudable Employments, that can engage the Attention of Man. – It is productive of numberless Blessings to Society, and is the Source that gives Birth, to all Manufactures and Commerce'.

From time to time leading landowners organised agricultural shows to demonstrate the latest 'improvements' and to disseminate information about them. At Woburn Abbey in June 1801 the Duke of Bedford, a noted enthusiast in the cause, held his annual sheep-shearing. It was attended by over five hundred agriculturists, including many noblemen, and lasted for three days. On the final day a large party, led by the Duke, proceeded to a fallow field at Crawley Farm where a number of implements were put through their paces:

> The instruments which attracted the most notice, and received the approbation of the best judges, were, a drilling machine, by Mr. Salmon, of Woburn, which was drawn by one horse, to drill seven rows of *any* kind of seed; and, if the horse went crooked, the man guiding the machine could keep it straight; ... Mr. Gooch's plough, from Northamptonshire, to plough deep or shallow, according to the soil ... and a drill, from Scotland .... . This lasted till near 4 o'clock, when, as

usual, near 300 retired to the Abbey, to partake of the Duke's hospitality.

The Gentleman's Magazine, Vol. LXXI,
Part 2 (1801), p.566.

Elsewhere, as in Jane Austen's *Sanditon*, the concern for 'improvement' might lead to the commercialisation of an estate. In this case Mr Parker, the owner, sought to exploit his property by creating a seaside resort.

> The success of Sanditon as a small, fashionable bathing place was the object, for which he seemed to live. A very few years ago, and it had been a quiet village of no pretensions; but some natural advantages in its position and some accidental circumstances having suggested to himself, and the other principal land holder, the probability of its becoming a profitable speculation, they had engaged in it, and planned and built, and praised and puffed, and raised it to a something of young renown – and Mr. Parker could now think of very little besides. . . .
>
> The village contained little more than cottages, but the spirit of the day had been caught, as Mr. Parker observed . . . , and two or three of the best of them were smartened up with a white curtain and 'Lodgings to let' –, and farther on, in the little green court of an old farm house, two females in elegant white were actually to be seen with their books and camp stools – and in turning the corner of the baker's shop, the sound of a harp might be heard through the upper casement.

Jane Austen *Sanditon* (1925), pp.161-62; 172.

Elsewhere a minority of landowners invested in the new economic infrastructure, such as canals and docks, or, like the Duke of Northumberland and Earl Fitzwilliam, exploited mineral deposits upon their estates. Others again made large fortunes from urban development in London and similar fast-growing centres.

But often it was merely a desire to embellish the appearance of their houses and gardens which absorbed the attention of owners. Properties were built or altered according to the fashionable Palladian (and later, Gothic) architectural style, while mansions were surrounded by landscaped parks and gardens designed by specialists like 'Capability' Brown, Humphry Repton, Nathaniel Kent and others. For Repton the dimensions of the parkland ought to 'bear some proportion to the command of property by which the mansion is supported . . . . Where the house itself is so situated as not to be much seen from the surrounding neighbourhood, it is the more necessary that some conspicuous object should mark a command of property'. (Quoted in Lawrence Stone and Jeanne C. Fawtier Stone, *An Open Elite? England 1540-1880*, p.336.) Yet this approach had its critics, including Fanny Price in *Mansfield Park*. She disliked the wholesale transformation of the landscape which these grandiose schemes entailed and favoured instead a more naturalistic approach to the picturesque. It seems that Jane Austen, as a member of a traditional gentry family, shared some of Fanny's doubts on the subject. Hence her mockery of the foolish Mr Rushworth, who desired to change his hitherto neglected estate of Sotherton into something which more nearly conformed to the current mode:

> Mr. Rushworth, . . . was now making his appearance at Mansfield, for the first time since the Crawfords' arrival. He had been visiting a friend in a neighbouring county, and that friend having recently had his grounds laid out by an improver, Mr. Rushworth was returned with his head full of the subject, and very eager to be improving his own place in the same way; and though not saying much to the purpose, could talk of nothing else. The subject had been already handled in the drawing-room; it was revived in the dining-parlour. . . .
>
> 'I wish you could see Compton,' said he, 'it is the most complete thing! I never saw a place so altered in my life. I told Smith I did not know where I was. The approach *now* is one of the finest things in the country. You see the house in the most surprising manner. I

declare when I got back to Sotherton yesterday, it looked like a prison – quite a dismal old prison.'

'Oh! for shame!' cried Mrs. Norris. 'A prison, indeed! Sotherton Court is the noblest old place in the world.'

'It wants improvement, ma'am, beyond any thing. I never saw a place that wanted so much improvement in my life; and it is so forlorn, that I do not know what can be done with it.'

'No wonder that Mr. Rushworth should think so at present,' said Mrs. Grant to Mrs. Norris, with a smile; 'but depend upon it, Sotherton will have *every* improvement in time which his heart can desire.'

'I must try to do something with it,' said Mr. Rushworth, 'but I do not know what. I hope I shall have some good friend to help me.'

'Your best friend upon such an occasion,' said Miss Bertram, calmly, 'would be Mr. Repton, I imagine.'

'That is what I was thinking of. As he has done so well by Smith, I think I had better have him at once. His terms are five guineas a day.'

'Well, and if they were *ten*,' cried Mrs. Norris, 'I am sure *you* need not regard it. The expense need not be any impediment. If I were you, I should not think of the expense. I would have every thing done in the best style, and made as nice as possible. Such a place as Sotherton Court deserves every thing that taste and money can do . . . .' . . .

Mr. Rushworth, however, though not usually a great talker, had still more to say on the subject next his heart. 'Smith has not much above a hundred acres altogether in his grounds, which is little enough, and makes it more surprising that the place can have been so improved. Now, at Sotherton, we have a good seven hundred, without reckoning the water meadows; so that I think, if so much could be done at Compton, we need not despair. There have been two or three fine old trees cut down that grew too near the house, and it opens the prospect amazingly, which makes me think that Repton, or any body of that sort, would certainly

> have the avenue at Sotherton down; the avenue that
> leads from the west front to the top of the hill, you
> know,' turning to Miss Bertram particularly as he
> spoke. . . .
> Fanny, who was sitting on the other side of Edmund
> . . . now looked at him, and said in a low voice,
> 'Cut down an avenue! What a pity! Does not it make
> you think of Cowper? "Ye fallen avenues, once more I
> mourn your fate unmerited." '
>
> Jane Austen, *Mansfield Park* (1813), pp.46-50.

Apparently more to Jane Austen's own taste was Mr
Knightley, the commonsense hero of *Emma*, who devoted his
time and attention to the running of his estate. Aware of the
responsibilities of his position, with a home farm, 'his sheep,
and his library, and all the parish to manage', he had little
opportunity for leisure. He regarded landownership as a trust,
and when his brother paid an annual Christmas visit the
conversation quickly turned to 'business matters':

> As a magistrate, he had generally some point of law to
> consult John about, or, at least, some curious anecdote
> to give; and as a farmer, as keeping in hand the
> home-farm at Donwell, he had to tell what every field
> was to bear next year, and to give all such local
> information as could not fail of being interesting to a
> brother whose home it had equally been the longest
> part of his life, and whose attachments were strong. The
> plan of a drain, the change of a fence, the felling of a tree,
> and the destination of every acre for wheat, turnips, or
> spring corn, was entered into with as much equality of
> interest by John, as his cooler manners rendered
> possible . . . .
>
> Jane Austen, *Emma* (1815), pp.90-91.

Mr Knightley exemplified the kind of landowner whom
many regarded as essential for the maintenance of a morally
founded, stable society. Colonel John Byng, the future Lord

Torrington (1743-1813) put forward much the same view about the duties of landowners in June 1794 when he commented disapprovingly upon the neglected state of the countryside around St Neots in Huntingdonshire. 'Surely,' he declared, 'it would be as beneficial to landlords as of utility to the State, to double the number of their farms, and to treble the number of their cottages – when their lands might be manured and crop'd – instead of laying as they do now, half drain'd, half till'd; the few people, and the few cattle seem nearly starv'd'. He went on to contrast bitterly the magnificent kennels erected for a duke's foxhounds with the

> miserable mud hovels erected for the sons of Adam; who looking, askance, with eyes of envy at the habitation of these happier hounds, regret their humanity and that they are not born fox hounds. It is from neglect, and despair that Democracy, that Anarchy, spring, would every landlord prove himself the guardian, the protector of his tenantry, who but would contribute to his sports, and preserve his game?
>
> But when the farmer is over rented, and the pauper finds himself without the habitation, or assistance given to dogs – flesh and blood will rebel: . . . whilst the unaided paupers of the country will look at a dog-kennell with envy; and the starvers of the town are to peep down, without hope upon the blazing displays of cookery – I will say *'Something is rotten in the State of Denmark'*.
>
> C. Bruyn Andrews and Fanny Andrews, eds, *The Torrington Diaries* (1954), pp.491; 494-95.

Later he condemned the failure to provide fuel and allotments for labouring people: 'Here is little fuel to be bought, little to be pick'd up, but that is punish'd as theft, no land allott'd them for potatoes, or ground for a cow: Agues devouring the children: . . . than these cottages . . . nothing can be more wretch'd; surround'd by hether (*sic*) they dare not collect, and by a profusion of turnips they dare not pluck'. (Ibid, p.506.)

Clearly not all landowners exercised their authority with

the consideration and care attributed to Mr Knightley and demanded by Colonel Byng. George Crabbe, in characteristically gloomy vein, described the atmosphere of decay and misery which could overhang a rural community where the principal landowner was non-resident and thus largely unaware of the needs of parishioners. And despite Crabbe's natural pessimistic tendencies, there is ample factual evidence that when landlords did live away from their estates, they were increasingly inclined to regard such properties as sources of revenue rather than as organic communities in their own right.

> Next died the Lady who yon Hall possess'd;
> And here they brought her noble bones to rest.
> In Town she dwelt; – forsaken stood the Hall:
> Worms ate the floors, the tap'stry fled the wall;
> No fire the kitchen's cheerless grate display'd;
> No cheerful light the long-closed sash convey'd;

> ※   ※   ※

> To empty rooms the curious came no more,
> From empty cellars turn'd the angry poor,
> And surly beggars cursed the ever-bolted door.
> To one small room the steward found his way,
> Where tenants follow'd to complain and pay;
> Yet no complaint before the Lady came,
> The feeling servant spared the feeble dame;
> Who saw her farms with his observing eyes,
> And answer'd all requests with his replies.
> She came not down, her falling groves to view;
> Why should she know, what one so faithful knew?
> Why come, from many clamorous tongues to hear,
> What one so just might whisper in her ear?
> Her oaks or acres why with care explore;
> Why learn the wants, the sufferings of the poor;
> When one so knowing all their worth could trace,
> And one so piteous govern'd in her place?

Lo! now, what dismal sons of Darkness come,
To bear this daughter of Indulgence home; . . . .

George Crabbe, *The Parish Register* (1807), Part
III, ll.233-38; 243-61.

Of a very different calibre was Lady Catherine De Bourgh.
On her estate at Hunsford she dominated not only the villagers
but the impressionable clergyman, Mr Collins, his wife, and
their guests:

> From the entrance hall, of which Mr. Collins pointed
> out, with a rapturous air, the fine proportion and
> finished ornaments, they followed the servants through
> an anti-chamber, to the room where Lady Catherine,
> her daughter, and Mrs. Jenkinson were sitting. – Her
> Ladyship, with great condescension, arose to receive
> them; . . . .
> The dinner was exceedingly handsome, and there
> were all the servants, and all the articles of plate which
> Mr. Collins had promised; and, as he had likewise
> foretold, he took his seat at the bottom of the table, by
> her ladyship's desire, and looked as if he felt that life
> could furnish nothing greater. . . .
> When the ladies returned to the drawing room, there
> was little to be done but to hear Lady Catherine talk,
> which she did without any intermission till coffee came
> in, delivering her opinion on every subject in so decisive
> a manner as proved that she was not used to have her
> judgment controverted. She enquired into Charlotte's
> domestic concerns familiarly and minutely, and gave
> her a great deal of advice, as to the management of them
> all; told her how every thing ought to be regulated in so
> small a family as her's, and instructed her as to the care
> of her cows and her poultry. Elizabeth found that
> nothing was beneath this great Lady's attention, which
> could furnish her with an occasion of dictating to
> others. . . .
> Elizabeth soon perceived that though this great Lady
> was not in the commission of the peace for the county,

she was a most active magistrate in her own parish, the minutest concerns of which were carried to her by Mr. Collins; and whenever any of the cottagers were disposed to be quarrelsome, discontented or too poor, she sallied forth into the village to settle their differences, silence their complaints, and scold them into harmony and plenty.

Jane Austen, *Pride and Prejudice* (1813),
pp.144-46; 150-51.

Yet, given this overweening power and influence of the major landholders, it is important to remember that over the greater part of England and Wales 'close' parishes like Hunsford, with one major landowner, were not typical. In 'open' villages, where ownership was more widely dispersed, a greater independence was possible. In Suffolk and Essex, for example, where the land had long been enclosed, yeomen farmers continued to flourish, while in the Vale of Pickering in Yorkshire, the agricultural writer, William Marshall, considered that there was probably no part of the kingdom which contained 'so great a number of *farms*, or rather parcels of land in distinct occupation'. In the township of Pickering alone there were about three hundred freeholders.

Westmorland, too, had many small proprietors, or 'statesmen' as they were called, eking out a meagre livelihood by dint of hard work and relentless economy. 'Their little tract of land serves as a kind of permanent rallying point for their domestic feelings', wrote Wordsworth in 1801. And it was with such sentiments in mind that he wrote of the stalwart Grasmere shepherd, Michael. Yet, in the end, Michael, like many of his fellow small proprietors, was forced to send his only son out into the world, a step which led ultimately to the lad's downfall. It was symptomatic of the financial pressures faced by small owners everywhere, especially after 1815, but before that date, too, in some districts.

Upon the forest-side in Grasmere Vale
There dwelt a Shepherd, Michael was his name;
An old man, stout of heart, and strong of limb.
His bodily frame had been from youth to age

Of an unusual strength: his mind was keen,
Intense, and frugal, apt for all affairs,
And in his shepherd's calling he was prompt
And watchful more than ordinary men . . . .

*   *   *

His days had not been passed in singleness.
His Helpmate was a comely matron, old –
Though younger than himself full twenty years.
She was a woman of a stirring life,
Whose heart was in her house: two wheels she had
Of antique form; this large, for spinning wool;
That small, for flax; and if one wheel had rest,
It was because the other was at work.
The Pair had but one inmate in their house,
An only Child, who had been born to them
When Michael, telling o'er his years, began
To deem that he was old, ...

*   *   *

I may truly say,
That they were as a proverb in the vale
For endless industry. When day was gone,
And from their occupations out of doors
The Son and Father were come home, even then,
Their labour did not cease; unless when all
Turned to the cleanly supper-board, and there,
Each with a mess of pottage and skimmed milk,
Sat round the basket piled with oaten cakes,
And their plain home-made cheese. Yet when the meal
Was ended, Luke (for so the Son was named)
And his old Father both betook themselves
To such convenient work as might employ
Their hands by the fire-side; perhaps to card
Wool for the Housewife's spindle, or repair
Some injury done to sickle, flail, or scythe,
Or other implement of house or field.

William Wordsworth, *Michael* (1800), ll.40-47;
78-89; 93-109.

Elsewhere some cottagers continued to have access to land for their livestock, perhaps by grazing them upon the commons or through squatter encroachments on forest or wasteland. But where these peasant cultivators survived they were often condemned as inefficient idlers or potential poachers. John Billingsley, an active agricultural improver and author of the *General View of the Agriculture of Somerset* (1794), stressed this aspect when he noted how much more productive the land would become if it were enclosed and a cost-conscious approach to farming adopted:

> moral effects of an injurious tendency accrue to the cottager, from a reliance on the imaginary benefits of stocking a common. The possession of a cow or two, with a hog, and a few geese, naturally exalts the peasant in his own conception above his brethren in the same rank of society. It inspires some degree of confidence in a property, inadequate to his support. In sauntering after his cattle, he acquires a habit of indolence. Quarter, half and occasionally whole days are imperceptibly lost. Day-labour becomes disgusting; the aversion increases by indulgence and, at length, the sale of a half-fed calf, or hog, finishes the means of adding intemperance to idleness.
>
> Quoted in J.H. Bettey, *Rural Life in Wessex 1500-1900*, p.36.

Although the complaints had a germ of truth in them, one feels that the greatest fault of these small cultivators was that they did not conform to the pattern of a desired rural hierarchy. It was that which most offended their critics. And it was under the influence of comments such as these, and of evidence of the greater profitability which attended changed practices, that the enclosure movement gained momentum, especially during the years of war with France.

Parliamentary Enclosure and Food Production: 1793-1815

Both in its own day and later the parliamentary enclosure movement proved controversial. Perhaps half of England had already been enclosed before it came to prominence in the middle of the eighteenth century. In some areas open fields had never existed, and in others they had been long eliminated by agreement or private arrangement. Over half of the land in Lincolnshire and Leicestershire, for example, had been enclosed before 1750. Nevertheless, it was after that date that parliamentary enclosure awards became significant, with over a thousand acts passed between 1760 and 1800, and a further eight hundred between 1800 and 1815. By contrast a mere 130 parliamentary awards had been on the statute book prior to 1760. (Peter Mathias, *The First Industrial Nation* (1983), p.67.) In all, perhaps seven million acres were covered by parliamentary enclosure awards between 1760 and 1815.

The movement's supporters claimed that it encouraged more efficient farming methods, thereby increasing food production and providing additional employment for hedgers, ditchers and other agricultural workers in the newly divided fields. Certainly food output was increased over the period, with estimated corn production rising from around fifteen million quarters in 1750 to about nineteen million by 1800 and twenty-five million by 1820. The soil was used more intensively, as former headlands and other common walkways were eliminated, and the larger, more compact fields were better cultivated. The landscape itself was transformed, as the strip cultivation in the large open fields of the lowland areas was exchanged for post and rail fences and quickset hedges around separate plots. In the uplands it was dry stone walls which broke up the former massive expanses of the old field systems.

In some counties, including Cambridgeshire, parts of Lincolnshire and the Midlands, enclosure meant converting a village's common land and arable open fields into individual holdings, with new farmhouses constructed among the fields, remote from the ancient centre of the village. In other cases, as in Cheshire, Cumbria and Yorkshire, it could mean the taking-in of land from the waste in order to create additional farmsteads, while occasionally, as on the heavy clay soils of Suffolk, former dairy pastures were ploughed to make way for grain growing. But whatever the regional pattern, the main aim was the same – to raise crop yields and improve the quality of farm livestock. During the years of scarcity in the Napoleonic Wars these pressures to raise productivity were intensified. It was also argued that the intermixed flocks and herds of numerous small owners, grazing upon common or unenclosed areas, encouraged the spread of disease and perpetuated inferior livestock strains. Nevertheless, many villagers, like the Northamptonshire labourer poet, John Clare, viewed the changes with deep hostility:

> There once were lanes in nature's freedom dropt,
> There once were paths that every valley wound –
> Inclosure came, and every path was stopt;
> Each tyrant fix'd his sign where paths were found,
> To hint a trespass now who cross'd the ground:
> Justice is made to speak as they command;
> The high road now must be each stinted bound:
> – Inclosure, thou'rt a curse upon the land,
> And tasteless was the wretch who thy existence plann'd.
>
> John Clare, *The Village Minstrel* (1821), ll.847-55.

To Goldsmith the changes deprived the peasant producer of the precarious independence he had hitherto enjoyed:

> Where then, ah! where, shall poverty reside,
> To 'scape the pressure of contiguous pride?
> If to some common's fenceless limits strayed,
> He drives his flock to pick the scanty blade,
> Those fenceless fields the sons of wealth divide,
> And even the bare-worn common is denied.
>
> Oliver Goldsmith, *The Deserted Village* (1770),
> ll.303-308.

Others, however, stressed the great material benefits that could accrue. Among them was the Carmarthenshire poet, John Dyer (c.1701-1758), an early enthusiast for enclosure, who became incumbent of Coningsby, Lincolnshire, in 1751. It was here that he penned the following lines, published in the year before his death:

But lightest wool is theirs who poorly toil
Thro' a dull round in unimproving farms
Of common fields. Inclose, inclose, ye Swains!
Why will you joy in common field, where pitch,
Noxious to wool, must stain your motley flock,
To mark your property? the mark dilates,
Enters the flake depreciated, defil'd,
Unfit for beauteous tint. Besides, in fields
Promiscuous held all culture languishes;
The glebe, exhausted, thin supply receives;
Dull waters rest upon the rushy flats
And barren furrows: none the rising grove
There plants for late posterity, nor hedge
To shield the flock, nor copse for cheering fire;
And in the distant village every hearth
Devours the grassy sward, the verdant food
Of injur'd herds and flocks, or what the plough
Should turn and moulder for the bearded grain:
Pernicious habit! drawing gradual on
Increasing beggary, and Nature's frowns.
Add too, the idle pilf'rer easier there
Eludes detection, when a lamb or ewe
From intermingled flocks he steals; or when,
With loosen'd tether of his horse or cow,
The milky stalk of the tall green-ear'd corn,
The year's slow rip'ning fruit, the anxious hope
Of his laborious neighbour, he destroys.

John Dyer, *The Fleece* (1757), Book II, ll.107-33.

The agricultural writer, William Marshall, likewise stressed the improved output which could follow from enclosure, as well as the enhanced value of the land which resulted:

Open lands, tho wholly appropriated, and lying well together, are of much less value, except for a sheep walk or a rabbit warren, than the same land would be in a state of suitable inclosure. If they are disjointed and intermixt in a *state of common field*, or *common meadow*, their value may be reduced one third. If the

common fields or meadows are what is termed *Lammas
land*, and become common as soon as the crops are off,
the depression of value may be set down at one half of
what they would be worth, in well fenced inclosures,
and unencumbered with that ancient custom . . . .

William Marshall, *On The Landed Property of
England* (1804), p.13.

Elsewhere he described unstinted commons, left virtually as
Nature had created them, as 'filthy blotches on the face of the
country: especially when seen under the threatening clouds of
famine which have now repeatedly overspread it.' (William
Marshall, *On the Appropriation and Inclosure of Commonable
and Intermixed Lands* (1801), p.12.)

However, among a number of otherwise favourable
observers there was growing concern at the social implications
of the enclosure movement. Detractors pointed to the loss of
traditional rights which often followed the enclosing of
commons and wasteland, and the heavy legal, fencing and
other costs which accompanied the reallocation of land
holdings. Both effects were particularly hard upon smaller
men. And, interestingly, recent research has confirmed that
although enclosure did not cause the elimination of small
owners, it could lead to sharp changes in the personnel
involved. In certain Buckinghamshire parishes enclosed
between 1780 and 1820 there was a decline of perhaps 40 to 50
per cent in the original owners. Admittedly, some of those
disappearing may also have been tenants, perhaps resident in
another village, who had sold their allocation in order to raise
capital to run a rented holding more efficiently, but others,
who had been on the fringes of yeoman status, were reduced
to the ranks of wage labourers under the new regime.
Significantly, Arthur Young, who had enthusiastically
declared in 1771, that 'provided open lands are enclosed, it is
not of very great consequence by what means it [is] effected',
was expressing serious doubts thirty years later. Although still
in favour of the movement for its economic benefits, he had
become convinced that, as hitherto carried out, it had resulted
in injustice to the poor. 'The fact is, that by nineteen enclosure

bills in twenty they are injured, in some grossly injured', he declared. And again: 'I had rather that all the commons of England were sunk in the sea, than that the poor should in future be treated on enclosing as they have generally been hitherto'. These factors and the consolidation of land into larger farming units were condemned still more severely by the rector of Barkham, Berkshire, David Davies:

> The depriving the peasantry of all landed property has beggared multitudes. It is plainly agreeable to sound policy, that as many individuals as possible in a state should possess an interest in the soil; because this attaches them strongly to the country and its constitution, and makes them zealous and resolute in defending them. . . . Formerly many of the lower sort of people occupied tenements of their own, with parcels of land about them, or they rented such of others. On these they raised for themselves a considerable part of their subsistence, without being obliged, as now, to buy all they want at shops. And this kept numbers from coming to the parish. But since those small parcels of ground have been swallowed up in the contiguous farms and inclosures, and the cottages themselves have been pulled down; the families which used to occupy them are crouded together in decayed farm-houses, with hardly ground enough about them for a cabbage garden: and being thus reduced to be *mere* hirelings, they are of course very liable to come to want. . . .
>
> It will perhaps be said, that numberless acts of inclosure have passed of late years; and that our agriculture has been continually advancing along with our other improvements. Let this be admitted: yet . . . as to the numerous inclosures that have been made, I fear the acts themselves will shew, that, in making them, too little regard has been paid to the encouragement and employment of labouring people.

David Davies, *The Case of Labourers in Husbandry Stated and Considered* (1795), pp.56; 81.

Food Shortages and Harvest Failures: 1793-1815

To add to the hardships created for labouring families by
war-time inflation, enclosure upheavals and the demands of
government for men and materials to pursue its military
objectives, there was the misery caused by repeated harvest
failures. Grain prices rose steeply in 1795-96, 1799-1801 and
1809-12 on this account, with the highest prices of the
nineteenth century reached in 1812. At that date wheat was
sold at 29s. 6d. a hundredweight and barley at 18s. 8d.; in 1793,
at the onset of the war, the respective prices had been 11s. 6d.
and 8s. 8d. From 1795 coarser quality bread only was to be
produced, to ensure maximum extraction of flour from a given
quantity of grain, and even the system of poor relief was
amended to take account of the higher bread prices. Individual
landowners played their part, too, by providing food for the
needy and by pressing local farmers to bring grain to market
instead of hoarding it in the hope that prices would rise still
higher. *Jackson's Oxford Journal* of 12 September 1795
reported with evident satisfaction the action of a Yorkshire
landlord who had given notice to quit to forty of his tenants
'upon proof that at the time of the greatest scarcity they were
hoarding up their corn'.

Typical of the charitable gestures made by owners and their
agents at this time were those on the Wrest Park estate,
Bedfordshire, where the agent informed his employer, Lady
Lucas, that he had bought 'a Barrell of Scotts Herrings . . . last
week, and the *Poor* are very *thankfull* for them at *A farthing
Each* & I have had a 2ᵈ· Barrell down last night by the Waggon
and if they go off Readily, I will have one Every week, for three
or four weeks to come; a Barrell contains *12* Hundred
Herrings and Cost rather more than a Halfpenny Each'. (29
March 1801.) In the previous year a still more comprehensive
programme had been inaugurated:

> I . . . have directed the keeper to kill the 3 brace of
> *Old-does*, and give them among the most distress[ed]
> Poor ... . A meeting of the Parishioners has been held
> and it has been unanimously agreed to give all the
> Laboring Poor *Six pence a Head* for each Child *a week*

under the age of 10 Years, so that a Labourer with 4 Children Receives from his Master 9ˢ· and 2ˢ· from the Parish together *11ˢ· a Week* – This is a plan more generally adopted in the County than any other, I found they had adopted it at Harrold, when I was there last week. In some places they agree and Buy Barley and Grind it, and Sell it to the Poor at 5ˢ· a Bushell, and the Loss made up by the Parish. The Potatoes which your Ladyship saw near Braberry Wood were a few the keeper had planted for his Family, he expected *20* Bushells, but when he dug them up they only produced 8 Bushells & the Poor people had stolen about 7 or 8 more . . . .

I will now only observe upon your Ladyships goodness [in] kindly allowing me to subscribe 10 Guineas for your Ladyship to the Poor.

Lucas MSS at Bedfordshire Record Office, L.30/ 11/215 ff.86 and 110, 19 January 1800.

These charitable gestures and changes in poor relief methods, did not prevent some labouring people from taking matters into their own hands when things became desperate. Food riots were a feature of eighteenth-century life even under less stringent conditions than these severe shortages. They normally had three principal objectives. First, they sought to press farmers and millers, who held grain, to bring it to market. Secondly, they attempted to stop the movement of food from one part of the country to another; this applied especially during the months of greatest scarcity, when some larger towns extended their catchment areas beyond their normal limits and small communities feared they would run short in consequence. Thirdly, they might seek to establish what was deemed a 'fair price' at which food would be sold in the market place. This happened particularly in country towns, where community ties were strong and there was a dependence on outside supplies of food. There was a widespread belief in the 'just price', and this led to bitter resentment when producers seemed to be abusing their bargaining power in times of distress by raising charges. Out of almost five hundred riots of various kinds which took place in provincial areas between 1790 and 1810, and which have recently been analysed by John Bohstedt, 48 per cent were concerned with food. Yet even in the worst years violent outbreaks were comparatively rare. Rural labourers, in particular, were unlikely to take part in such disturbances unless another group such as colliers or clothworkers provided the lead. This seems to have been partly due to timidity and lack of confidence in their own powers, but it can also be attributed to the greater availability of food in the villages. True the *potential* threat of unrest was present, but those in authority were usually sufficiently sensitive to the dangers of the situation not to allow matters to get seriously out of hand. Magistrates combined force with conciliation, varying their tactics as circumstances demanded, and calling upon the help of the military or special constables to quell the most serious disturbances. Significantly the response to extensive rioting in Devon market towns in 1801 was the creation of a thorough and sophisticated county relief programme, designed to end 'apprehension of further distress'.

The alarm felt by JPs and other members of the propertied classes is shown clearly in the letters they sent to the Home Secretary, detailing the discontent in their area and, often enough, asking for soldiers to be sent to prevent the situation worsening. Thus Thomas Griffith, a Flint magistrate, wrote to the Home Secretary on 2 April 1795:

> Different Mobs in considerable numbers have repeatedly assembled in different parts, upon the Plea of the high price of corn. Hitherto they have been talked into tolerable order by the interference of the Magistrates, but how long this may have effect is difficult to guess.
>
> As yet no very material Injury has been done. The greatest violence used was at Mold, where they broke open the Ware house of a Man, who buys Corn in this County for the use of Cheshire and Lancashire, and forced him to sell it to them somewhat under the market price. But had they taken it for nothing they were in too

great strength for us to have attempted to oppose with the civil Power only. Our Request therefore is, (for I write in the names of several Magistrates) that some Troops may be quartered within our reach. At present there are none in this County or near it, and should the numerous Body of Colliers and Miners again assemble, the property of the whole Country might be laid waste and destroy'd before Assistance could be procured.

> Home Office Correspondence, 1795, at Public Record Office, H.O. 42/34/280.

Similarly, the diary entries of Mary Hardy, a farmer's wife from Letheringsett, near Holt, Norfolk, show that during December 1795, poor people had seized five loads of flour at nearby Sharrington as it was on its way to Kings Lynn for shipment out of the county.

> *Dec. 18*: A great many people gathered together there unloaded the flower and sett it in a house. The Justices could not persuade them to give it up.
> *Dec. 19*: The Justices sat [a] great part of the day to settle the mob, but nothing was done and no other business was transacted. They sent for a Troop of Horse from Norwich and a party of Foot Soldiers from Aylsham. They arrived at Holt abt. 8 o'c. on Sunday morng.
> *Dec. 20 (Sun.)*: The Soldiers marched thro our town about 10 o'clock went to Sherington (*sic*) and set a guard over the flower that was seized took up a man named Bone suposed to be one of the ringleaders of the mob. . . .
> *Dec. 21*: A very wet day. The soldiers and Justices and a large party of farmers went through the town morng 11 to Sherington and guarded the flower which was seized as far as Stock Heath. Mr. Hardy went with them part of the way, came back to dinner.

> B. Cozens-Hardy (ed.), *Mary Hardy's Diary* (1968), pp.90-91. (Diary covers the period 1773-1809.)

As large grain producers the Hardy family were naturally concerned at the seizure of the flour. But it will be noted that, despite the fears expressed, the 'mob' was quickly put down. This was the general experience.

Furthermore, despite the extensive literature which has emerged upon food riots in recent years, this should not lead to the assumption that violent outbreaks were common, even in the most difficult periods. Far more typical of the daily round of most labouring men was that depicted by Robert Bloomfield in *The Farmer's Boy* (1800). Bloomfield, a tailor's son from Honington, Suffolk, was born in 1766. Following his father's death, Mrs Bloomfield combined running a small dame school with work as a wool spinster in order to maintain her family, until her remarriage in 1773 after six years of widowhood. When Robert was eleven, he began working as a farmer's boy for an uncle by marriage. He remained at the job four years, before following his two elder brothers to London, where they worked as shoemakers. It was that occupation which he himself subsequently took up. *The Farmer's Boy* was composed in a spirit of nostalgia for the country life of the poet's youth, as well as, perhaps, a desire to satisfy the romantic imaginings of the work's assumed middle and upper-class readership. It was divided into four sections, to correspond to the four seasons. The first extract is from 'Summer':

> Here, midst the boldest triumphs of her worth,
> Nature herself invites the reapers forth;
> Dares the keen sickle from its twelvemonth's rest,
> And gives that ardour which in every breast
> From infancy to age alike appears,
> When the first sheaf its plumy top uprears.
> No rake takes here what Heaven to all bestows –
> Children of want, for you the bounty flows!
> And every cottage from the plenteous store
> Receives a burden nightly at its door.
>
> Hark! where the sweeping scythe now rips along
> Each sturdy Mower, emulous and strong,

Whose writhing form meridian heat defies,
Bends o'er his work, and every sinew tries;
Prostrates the waving treasure at his feet,
But spares the rising clover, short and sweet,
Come Health! come, Jollity! light-footed, come;
Here hold your revels, and make this your home.

> ✳   ✳   ✳

Th' unpeopled dwelling mourns its tenants stray'd;
E'en the domestic, laughing Dairy-Maid
Hies to the Field, the general toil to share.
Meanwhile the Farmer quits his elbow-chair,
His cool brick-floor, his pitcher, and his ease,
And braves the sultry beams, and gladly sees
His gates thrown open, and his team abroad,
The ready group attendant on his word,
To turn the swarth, the quiv'ring load to rear,
Or ply the busy rake, the land to clear.

> ✳   ✳   ✳

Now noon gone by, and four declining hours,
The weary limbs relax their boasted pow'rs;
Thirst rages strong, the fainting spirits fail,
And ask the sov'reign cordial, home-brew'd ale:
Beneath some shelt'ring heap of yellow corn
Rests the hoop'd keg, and friendly cooling horn,
That mocks alike the goblet's brittle frame,
Its costlier potions, and its nobler name.

Robert Bloomfield, *The Farmer's Boy* (1800),
'Summer' ll.131-48; 151-60; 181-88.

A very different atmosphere is conjured up by 'Autumn', with Giles, the farmer's boy, expected to share in the laborious duties of tillage, alongside the older men:

For searching frosts and various ills invade,
Whilst wintry months depress the springing blade.

The plough moves heavily, and strong the soil,
And clogging harrows with augmented toil
Dive deep: and clinging, mixes with the mould
A fatt'ning treasure from the nightly fold,
And all the cow-yard's highly valu'd store,
That late bestrew'd the blacken'd surface o'er.

*   *   *

Here Giles for hours of indolence atones
With strong exertion, and with weary bones,
And knows no leisure; till the distant chime
Of Sabbath bells he hears at sermon time,
That down the brook sound sweetly in the gale,
Or strike the rising hill, or skim the dale.

Robert Bloomfield, *The Farmer's Boy* (1800),
'Autumn', ll.59-66; 71-76.

The Alarms of the French War Period

The wars with revolutionary France extended from 1793 to
1815 and involved the recruitment of large numbers of men for
the armed forces. Perhaps one in every six adult males was
engaged in the hostilities, either by land or sea, and there were
almost half a million men under arms in 1815 alone (two-thirds
of them in the army). They included Irishmen, Hanoverians
and foreign mercenaries, as well as recruits from Britain itself,
many of whom came from rural districts. In some communities
the exodus of the men created temporary shortages of farm
labour which could only be met by the greater use of migrant
workers and of women and children. More than a century later
there was a tradition on the Berkshire Downs of the 'petticoat'
harvests during the Napoleonic Wars, when the women
brought in most of the grain. Machinery, too, particularly
threshing machines, came into wider use during this period.
    There were repeated fears of a French invasion, which

reached peaks in 1797-98 and 1803, and aroused deep anxiety in many rural communities. In some cases contingency arrangements were sanctioned to evacuate the infirm, the sick and the women and children from coastal districts should the need arise. Livestock was also to be removed beyond the reach of potential invaders, as plans drawn up in Essex during 1803 make clear:

> That in case of Invasion all Horses & Draft Cattle that cannot be driven out of the reach of the Enemy be shot; and that the Axle Trees or Wheels of all Carriages likely to fall into the Enemy's hands be broken: the fullest Assurance being given of complete Indemnification provided no Horses, Draft Cattle or Carriages fall into the Enemy's hands thro' negligence or want of proper exertion on the part of the Owners.
>
> All other Stock is to be left for the use of the Troops unless there be evident danger it may fall into the Enemy's hands, in which case the measures formerly determined upon must be resorted to.
>
> Arthur Young, MSS at the British Library, Add. MSS 35, 129, f.78, letter dated 8 December 1803.

The need to provide men, horses and tax-revenues to wage the war imposed heavy burdens on landowners and farmers, which went some way towards counterbalancing the benefits they enjoyed from rising rentals and high food prices. There was, however, a reluctance among many of the propertied classes to volunteer for service in the armed forces. Military duties were regarded by such unwilling recruits as inconvenient interruptions to the serious business of earning a living. Even the veteran officer, Colonel John Byng, who had served for almost a quarter of a century in the 1st Foot Guards, was opposed to a widespread campaign to draw men from the land: 'as an old soldier I am averse from militias', he wrote, 'and as a citizen I think it has sadly debauch'd the yeoman officer, and the peasant soldier: who return from campaigning into their own country, very different subjects from which they left it.' (C. Bruyn Andrews and Fanny Andrews (eds), *The Torrington Diaries* (1954), p.473.) About a month later, in June 1794, he gloomily added: 'Alas! I think I see the end of King by Government, and indeed of all rule, approaching! Hastily and unthinkingly plunged into war – discontent will increase with taxes – and we shall double our stakes like ruin'd gamesters.' (Ibid, p.491.)

Elizabeth Girling, a Norfolk farmer's daughter, noted that, although some of the village women were terrified at the prospect of an invasion during the summer and autumn of 1803, her own two brothers had resolved not to leave home 'till the French come'. In a letter to a third brother she commented:

> Most of the cavalry have volunteered themselves to go to Yarmouth for a week or a fortnight. The Norfolk Rangers were there last week, and used no better than common soldiers. They are obliged to get up at any time of the night if they hear the Bugle, and sometimes are taken six or seven miles by the seaside. . . . The talk is now that when they have once volunteered they can be sent anywhere. The people seem very much dissatisfied about it.
>
> 'George Paston', *Sidelights on the Georgian Period* (1902), p.247.

Jane Austen's novels, written for the most part during the war period, also display a surprising indifference to the hostilities. This lack of concern is reflected in her correspondence. Although she mentions periodically the careers of her two Royal Naval officer brothers, Francis and Charles, national events seemingly impinged but little upon her consciousness and still less upon her emotions. Typical of her cool response is a comment in a letter to her sister, Cassandra, concerning the death of Sir John Moore, the British commander in Spain:

> I am sorry to find that Sir J. Moore has a mother living, but tho' a very Heroick son, he might not be a very necessary one to her happiness, ... Thank Heaven!

we have had no one to care for particularly among the
Troops . . . . Col. Maitland is safe & well; his Mother
& sisters were of course anxious about him, but there is
no entering much into the solicitudes of that family.

R.W. Chapman (ed.), *Jane Austen's Letters*, 30
January 1809, pp.261-62.

In such circumstances resort was often had to privately
raised volunteers, especially to supply military requirements
on the home front. Among those involved in this particular
activity was the Northamptonshire farm-labourer poet, John
Clare. He was caught up in a project organised near his native
Helpstone, as he subsequently recounted tongue-in-cheek:

When the country was chin-deep in the fears of
invasion & every month was filled with the terrors
which Bonaparte had spread in other countries a
national scheme was set on foot to raise a raw army of
volunteers & to make the matter plausible a letter was
circulated said to be written by the prince regent I
forget how many was demanded from our parish but I
remember the panic which it created was very great . . .
the papers that were circulated assured the people of
England that the French were on the eve of invading it
& that it was deemed nessesary by the regent that an
army from 18 to 45 should be raised immediately this
was the great lye . . . little lies were soon at its heels
which assured the people of Helpstone that the French
had invaded & got to London & some of these little lyes
had the impudence to swear that the french had even
reached northampton the people got at their doors in
the evening to talk over the rebellion of '45 when the
rebels reached Derby & even listened at intervals to
fancy they heard the french 'rebels' at Northampton
knocking it down with their cannon I never gave much
credit to popular storys of any sort so I felt no concern
at these . . . though I coud not say much for my valour
if the tale had provd true we had a cross-graind sort of
choice left us which was to be forced to be drawn [to

enter the militia] & go for nothing or take on as volunteers for a bounty of two guineas I accepted the latter & went with a neighbours son W. Clarke to Peterbrough to be sworn in & prepard to join the regiment at Oundle the morning we left home our mothers parted with us as if we were going to Botany Bay & people got at their doors to bid us farewell & greet us with a Job's comfort that they doubted we should see Helpstone no more . . . when we got to Oundle the place of quartering we were drawn out into the fields & a more motley multitude of lawless fellows was never seen in Oundle before & hardly out of it there were 1300 of us we was drawn up into a line & sorted into companys . . . some took lodgings but lodgings were very expensive . . . so I was obligd to be content with the quarters alloted me which were at the Rose & Crown Inn . . . .

The officers were often talking about Bonaparte in the field & praising each other in a very ridiculous manner . . . .

On the last time we was calld up there was a fresh bounty set on foot of a further 2 guineas to those who woud enlist for extended service as they calld it to be sent so many miles out of the country to guard barracks castles or any other urgencys that might happen five shillings of which was to be paid down & the rest to be given when they were wanted . . . I felt purposes enew for the 5 shillings & when it was offerd me I took it without further enquirey & never heard further about it.

> J.W. and Anne Tibble (eds), *The Prose of John Clare*, pp.46-50. (Manuscript completed by Clare c.1826.)

The chaotic administration Clare experienced seems to have been typical of many volunteer forces and militia regiments. Colonel John Byng described members of the Derby Militia whom he met in May 1794 as 'dirty, and ill disciplined', while their Cambridge counterparts were condemned as 'neither well chosen nor well disciplined. Why can their officers belong to them without knowledge or zeal?' (C. Bruyn Andrews and Fanny Andrews eds, *The Torrington Diaries* (1954), pp.473, 481.) In such circumstances it was fortunate that tentative French invasion plans were never implemented.

3 The Post-war World, 1815-1840s

The decline of leases was but one facet of the altered agricultural situation after 1815 and the changes which this produced in the landowners' position. It is now generally recognized that 'the agricultural depression' did not exist as a period of general and persistent gloom, loss and stagnation for all farmers stretching unbroken from the end of the Napoleonic wars to a recovery miraculously timed to start with the accession of the young queen in 1837. There was a series of short crises affecting cereal farmers, associated with abundant harvests and low prices. . . . Stock and dairy farmers were affected by the crisis of the early 1820s, but otherwise had little cause for complaint.

F.M.L. Thompson, *English Landed Society in the Nineteenth Century* (1963), p.231.

The Countryside after the War

With the coming of peace in 1815, after almost a quarter of a century of conflict, there was a period of painful readjustment not only within British agriculture but within the economy as a whole. Men returning from the armed forces had to be reabsorbed into civilian employment and the manufacturing industry reorientated towards peacetime production. The continuing growth of the northern factory system also hit hard those engaged in the textile trade elsewhere. Significantly when riots broke out in East Anglia in 1816, as a protest against unemployment and low wages, displaced clothworkers were prominent among those taking part. In a letter to the Home Secretary written in April 1816, the Duke of Grafton, Lord

Lieutenant of Suffolk, attributed the riots and suffering in the Cosford Hundred of that county to the 'total failure of the spinning of long wool, which used to afford employment to so many thousand persons in this county'. (A.J. Peacock, *Bread or Blood* (1965), p.27.) That opinion was endorsed by magistrates meeting at Bury St Edmunds.

It was in this atmosphere of poverty and simmering discontent that Shelley issued his clarion cry to the 'Men of England', calling for the immediate introduction of economic and social reforms:

> Men of England, wherefore plough
> For the lords who lay ye low?
> Wherefore weave with toil and care
> The rich robes your tyrants wear?
>
>   ＊   ＊   ＊
>
> The seed ye sow, another reaps;
> The wealth ye find, another keeps;
> The robes ye weave, another wears;
> The arms ye forge, another bears.
>
>   ＊   ＊   ＊
>
> With plough and spade, with hoe and loom,
> Trace your grave, and build your tomb,
> And weave your winding-sheet, till fair
> England be your sepulchre.

> Percy Bysshe Shelley, *Song to the Men of England*
> (1819), ll.1-4; 17-20; 29-32.

Although there was no sustained resistance to these conditions on the lines he demanded, sporadic unrest, repressive legislation and financial hardship continued to mark the first years of peace.

Meanwhile it was among the farming community that some of the most difficult economic realities had to be faced. During the war both farmers and landowners had prospered, thanks to

the prevailing high food prices and high rentals which had
outstripped the rise in their respective annual expenditure. But
in 1813, with a better harvest, wheat prices fell sharply from the
crisis levels of 1809–12. The fall continued in 1814–15 and with
it came the successful demand by the landed interest for the
passage of the controversial 1815 Corn Law. This prohibited
the sale of foreign wheat on the British market until the home
price had reached 80s. a quarter. For barley and oats the
respective limits were set at 40s. and 27s. All were well above
pre-war prices and to consumers it seemed a policy designed to
benefit farmers and landowners at their expense. Byron joined
in the chorus of protest at the selfishness of the 'superior
orders':

> Alas, the country! how shall tongue or pen
> Bewail her now *un*country gentlemen?
> The last to bid the cry of warfare cease,
> The first to make a malady of peace.
> For what were all these country patriots born?
> To hunt, and vote, and raise the price of corn?

❈   ❈   ❈

> But where is now the goodly audit ale?
> The purse-proud tenant, never known to fail?
> The farm which never yet was left on hand?
> The marsh reclaim'd to most improving land?
> The impatient hope of the expiring lease?
> The doubling rental? What an evil's peace!
> In vain the prize excites the ploughman's skill,
> In vain the Commons pass their patriot bill;

❈   ❈   ❈

> The land self-interest groans from shore to shore,
> For fear that plenty should attain the poor.
> Up, up again, ye rents! exalt your notes,
> Or else the ministry will lose their votes,

❈   ❈   ❈

The peace has made one general malcontent
Of these high-market patriots; war was rent!
Their love of country, millions all mis-spent,
How reconcile? by reconciling rent!
And will they not repay the treasures lent?
No: down with every thing, and up with rent!

> Lord Byron, *The Age of Bronze* (1823), XIV,
> ll.1-6; 23-30; 33-36; 57-62.

Byron's known Radical opinions probably led most landowners to discount his vitriolic attack. But soon concern over the operation of the Corn Laws was to come from a different source, for it became obvious to the more perceptive agriculturists that the constant switching on and off of the import tap, to which protection led, and the variations in harvest yields in this country, which it could not influence, were aggravating the price fluctuations rather than preventing them. The situation was exacerbated by the fact that in 1821-23 Britain decided to end the war-time system of paper money and to return to pre-war gold standard arrangements. Under the deflationary governmental policies which followed, prices dropped even further.

The problems confronting farmers in the immediate aftermath of the war were highlighted in a survey conducted by the Board of Agriculture in 1816. Thus from Great Bealings in Suffolk Edward Moor wrote:

> As a magistrate for this county, heretofore so wealthy and happy, no day, scarcely no hour of any day, passes, without some occurrence bringing before me some instance of agricultural distress. ... Small farmers coming to parish officers for work – all classes of farmers employing more men than they want, and would employ if left to their own choice; though they can so ill afford this, it is better than maintaining able men to do nothing, and living upon the [poor] rates. ... Inability to pay rent and their current expenses are other circumstances denoting the distress of the farmers, who still hold their ground. Instead of

riding, they walk to market, where within short
distances – instead of dining at their clubs at their
different inns, many of them go home to dinner. I do
not note this as a distressing part, only as denoting a
feeling of the times. Few of those who do remain to
dine, drink wine, as they almost all did, until lately. This
is no great hardship, nor that their daughters come no
longer to the milliners or dancing masters, &c. who
have thus lost by far their best customers. Even
gentlemen of comfortable incomes (say from one to
two or three thousand a year) depending on the rents
and profits of land, are unable to pay their tradesmen's
bills. A medical man, in great practice, instead of
receiving 300 l. from the neighbouring *farmers*, as he
usually does, on account of his bills, at Christmas, did
not, this year, receive 20 l. In short, the pressure is very
great. I give it, as my opinion, not formed hastily, but
necessarily somewhat vaguely, that if the farmers of
Suffolk had, for the last year, had their farms rent free,
they would not have made any money of them. Labour,
taxes, tithe, and tradesmen's bills would, I think, have
absorbed the whole produce.

> *The Agricultural State of the Kingdom in February,*
> *March and April, 1816* (1816), pp.312-14.

Even the non-arable districts, although less acutely affected,
did not escape unscathed. A Devon man, for example, pointed
to the large number of untenanted farms around Kingsbridge:

The landlords unfortunately knowing very little of
agriculture, and being taken by surprise, have not the
means of managing their farms; and, consequently,
they are, in a great measure, uncultivated.

A number of tenants, to my knowledge, have given
notice to their landlords of quitting their farms . . . but
what is far more calamitous, the usual method, now-a-
day, among tenants, is not to give any notice, but
advertise all their stock to be sold by auction,
immediately before a quarter-day, pay up the rent to

that period, and then desert the farm, leaving the landlord the only remedy, of prosecuting on the lease (if any) if he chuses. And a considerable number of farmers, still more unprincipled, have driven off the whole of their cattle, and even removed their household furniture, and all their dead stock, [farm implements, &c.] by night, leaving the landlord without a remedy.

Ibid, pp.63-64.

Landowners responded, often belatedly, by reducing rentals or granting rent rebates. But some of the smaller men, who had themselves purchased properties at inflated war-time prices on borrowed money, were forced into bankruptcy by the sudden turn of events. The larger landholders had sufficient resources to meet the changes, however, and they were able not only to cut rents but to assume a greater responsibility for estate repairs. Although the process was not painless, most weathered the storm without too much difficulty and were able to engage in their favourite leisure pursuit of field sports. E.W. Bovill (*The England of Nimrod and Surtees 1815-1854* (1959), p.11) has even described this period as 'the golden age of foxhunting'. At the time of Waterloo, he declared, this was 'still little more than a private pastime of sporting squires. During the next forty years it ... became a great national sport'.

Cobbett, writing in 1821, took a less sanguine view. His attitude was partly coloured by his hatred of government policy – the wartime system of paper money, for example, and the widespread use of patronage, placemen, and pensioners – but partly it was a recognition of the undoubted short-term difficulties which existed:

As an instance of the change which rural customs have undergone since the hellish paper-system has been so furiously at work, I need only mention the fact, that, forty years ago, there were *five* packs of *fox-hounds* and *ten* packs of *harriers* kept within *ten miles* of Newbury; and that now there is *one* of the former (kept, too, by *subscription*) and *none* of the latter, except the few

couple of dogs kept by Mr. Budd! 'So much the better,'
says the shallow fool, who cannot duly estimate the
difference between a resident *native* gentry, attached to
the soil, known to every farmer and labourer from their
childhood, frequently mixing with them in those
pursuits where all artificial distinctions are lost,
practising hospitality without ceremony, from habit
and not on calculation; and a gentry, only now-and-
then residing at all, having no relish for country-
delights, foreign in their manners, distant and haughty
in their behaviour, looking to the soil only for its rents,
viewing it as a mere object of speculation, unacquainted
with its cultivators, despising them and their pursuits,
and relying, for influence, not upon the good will of the
vicinage, but upon the dread of their power. The war
and paper-system has brought in nabobs, negro-
drivers, generals, admirals, governors, commissaries,
contractors, pensioners, sinecurists, commissioners,
loan-jobbers, lottery-dealers, bankers, stock-jobbers;
not to mention the long and *black list* in gowns and
three-tailed wigs. You can see but few good houses not
in possession of one or the other of these. These, with
the parsons, are now the magistrates.

> William Cobbett, *Rural Rides*, Vol. I (1853),
> pp.37-38.

Almost a year later a visit to Weyhill Fair led to similar gloomy
comments:

The 11th of October is the Sheep-fair. About £300,000
used, some few years ago, to be carried home by the
sheep-sellers. To-day, less, perhaps, than £70,000, and
yet the *rents* of these sheep-sellers are, perhaps, as high,
on an average, as they were then. The countenances of
the farmers were descriptive of their ruinous states. I
never, in all my life, beheld a more mournful scene.
There is a horsefair upon another part of the down; and
there I saw horses keeping pace in depression with the
sheep. A pretty numerous group of the tax-eaters, from
Andover and the neighbourhood, were the only

persons that had smiles on their faces. I was struck with a young farmer trotting a horse backward and forward to show him off to a couple of gentlemen, who were bargaining for the horse, and one of whom finally purchased him. These *gentlemen* were two of our "*dead-weight*," and the horse was that on which the farmer had pranced in the *Yeomanry Troop*! Here is a turn of things! Distress; pressing distress; dread of the bailiffs alone could have made the farmer sell his horse. If he had the firmness to keep the tears out of his eyes, his heart must have paid the penalty. . . .

From this dismal scene, a scene formerly so joyous, we set off back to Uphusband pretty early . . . Met with a farmer who said he must be ruined, unless another 'good war' should come! This is no uncommon notion. They saw high prices *with* war, and they thought that the war was the *cause*.

Ibid, Vol. I, pp.116-17.

Among the labouring classes, meanwhile, the position was still more desperate, with widespread unemployment the order of the day and much resort to parish poor relief for subsistence. Joseph Mayett, a Buckinghamshire labourer, born at Quainton in March 1783, was one victim of these adverse conditions. In February 1803 he joined the army and continued to serve until his demobilisation early in 1815:

Having obtained my discharge from the army and being returned home I began to fancy myself that all my Troubles were at an end. I found myself among my own friends and those that I believed were real Christians . . . . [But] at Michaelmas my master declined business and I was out of work and I being a single man and at that time the King wanted Soldiers so the parish would not employ me but I was determined not to go for a soldier again so I set up to gather old raggs and sell a few things such as tapes, laces, thred (*sic*) and cotton &c. at which I done pretty well at first and still enjoyed my liberty on the 18th of Dec^r· I married . . . . I gave up gathering rags and took to work for which I received 7ˢ⁻ per week to maintain me and my wife and bread was 3ˢ⁻ per loaf in this Case I was much distressed but the summer Coming on I was soon relieved by an advance of wages but the harvest proved very wet so that I met with a disappoint[ment] by the great loss of time I sustained but after harvest I met with a place of work at the Esquire at 10ˢ⁻ per week and the price of bread was sunk to 2ˢ⁻ per loaf and by these means things of a temporal nature began to take a favorable turn . . . at this time the squire that I worked for had hired a Baily to manage the farm for him and in the month of January 1818 the esquire being gone out for a long time the baily took it upon himself to reduce the wages of me and several more of the men [who] had no Children for he said a man without a family could live better upon 9ˢ⁻ per week than those that [had] Children could upon 10ˢ⁻ but he required us to do as much work as they so in the month of March we all left him and got work else where . . . .

In the month of Jany. 1825 I was out of work and was compeled to go into a milking place again the Esquire that lived in the Parish and was a magistrate wanted a man that could milk and there being no other man out of work at that time beside me he set upon me and made me go or I should have no employ so I was forced to go or starve . . . .

Autobiography of Joseph Mayett, MS at
Buckinghamshire Record Office, D/X371.

A minority of farmers and labourers responded to the changed times by emigrating with their families, particularly to North America. According to one witness in the early 1830s, there was 'not a township, or hardly a family' in the North Riding of Yorkshire, 'but what had some of the inhabitants and some of their relations gone to America'. Even men with capital were going abroad in the belief that they could not 'do worse than they are doing at home, because they have been sinking so fast'. (Quoted in Pamela Horn, *The Rural World 1780-1850* (1980), p.75.) The activities of emigration societies and the publication of books and official government papers, recounting the experiences of British settlers in North America, all indicate the deep anxieties which existed in the farming community at this time.

Gradually, however, conditions began to improve. Among stock farmers, except for the recession of the early 1820s and an outbreak of disease among sheep in the last years of that decade, hardships were relatively slight. Overall demand for animal products was growing fast, as the rapidly expanding industrial towns increased their consumption of meat, butter, cheese and eggs. As a Cheshire land agent put it in 1833, it was the state of trade in industrial Lancashire which determined the prosperity of farmers and landowners in his part of the world: 'we always find when trade is good at Manchester, cheese and the produce of the farmer sells better'. (Quoted in Pamela Horn, *The Rural World 1780-1850*, p.77.) Even grain producers learned to adjust to the era of low prices and to alter their farming methods, so as to cut costs. Lower rentals and land improvement schemes also helped. In parts of Suffolk, for example, output was raised by better drainage and the use of new crop rotations, among other things.

From the late 1830s, too, population growth once more outstripped the rise in grain output and the country became an increasingly heavy importer of corn during years of both good and bad harvest. So, for farmers at least, if not for the urban consumer, the era of severe depression came to an end as the downward trend of prices was finally arrested. The reduction in poor-rate expenditure also helped in this direction, while agriculturists began to adopt more hard-headed commercial attitudes to the tillage of their holdings. Typical of this approach was Tennyson's *Northern Farmer: New Style*:

> Dosn't thou 'ear my 'erse's legs, as they canters awaäy?
> Proputty, proputty, proputty – that's what I 'ears 'em saäy.
> Proputty, proputty, proputty – Sam, thou's an ass for thy paaïns:
> Theer's moor sense i' one o' 'is legs nor in all thy braaïns.

*   *   *

Look thou theer wheer Wrigglesby beck cooms out by
the 'ill!
Feyther run oop to the farm, an' I runs oop to the mill;
An' I'll run oop to the brig, an' that thou'll live to see;
And if thou marries a good un I'll leäve the land to thee.

Thim's my noätions, Sammy, wheerby I means to stick;
But if thou marries a bad un, I'll leäve the land to Dick. –
Coom oop, proputty, proputty – that's what I 'ears 'im
saäy –
Proputty, proputty, proputty – canter an' canter
awaäy.

Alfred Tennyson, *Northern Farmer: New Style*
(1869), ll.1-4; 53-60.

Yet throughout the period many of the old traditions of
country life also continued, despite the disruptions and
disappointments. Migratory harvest gangs were still employed
on many holdings to help at the busiest times of the year, and
some of the migrants were able so to arrange their tasks that
they could move easily between home and host communities.
Thus during the 1830s men around Rotherfield in East Sussex
first went haymaking near London before returning home for
the corn-harvest. They then moved away for a second
corn-harvest in the hill-country around Lewes before
travelling northwards to end the season in the Kent and Surrey
hop gardens. A decade earlier Cobbett, writing from St
Albans, had commented on the haymaking gangs whom he had
encountered around London:

> From Kensington to this place, through Edgware,
> Stanmore, and Watford, the crop is almost entirely hay,
> from fields of permanent grass, manured by dung and
> other matter brought from the *Wen*. [*His name for
> London.*] Near the Wen, where they have had the *first
> haul* of the Irish and other perambulating labourers, the
> hay is all in rick. . . . It is curious to observe how the
> different labours are divided as to the *nations*. The
> mowers are all *English*; the haymakers all *Irish*.

William Cobbett, *Rural Rides*, Vol. 1 (1853), p.84.

Women's Employment

Women, too, played their part in the employment field. Although domestic service remained the biggest single recruiter of permanent female labour in country and town alike, there were certain areas where this did not apply. In the far north of England and in Wales permanent female workers on the land were common, while almost everywhere it was customary for women to lend a hand on the farms at the busy seasons of the year. Indeed, on most holdings the skill of the women in dairying and poultry management played a major part in the financial success of the whole enterprise, as the redoubtable Mrs Poyser in George Eliot's *Adam Bede* clearly demonstrated.

In other cases it was the survival of domestic industries which provided a prime outlet for females. Although the growth of the factory system, particularly from the 1780s, had undermined the prosperity of those engaged in cottage spinning and weaving, a few trades, like lacemaking, gloving and straw plaiting for the hat and bonnet trade, were able to withstand most of the pressures of mechanisation and to offer employment to domestic workers until the middle of the century.

Changes introduced under the 1834 Poor Law Amendment Act, which phased out many of the old allowances and tightened up conditions of poor relief, added to the pressures on women to work. In Sussex it was reported in 1835 that 'the custom of the mother of a family carrying her infant with her in its cradle into the field, rather than lose the opportunity of adding her earnings to the general stock, though partially practised before, is becoming very much more general now.' (Quoted in Ivy Pinchbeck, *Women Workers and the Industrial Revolution 1750-1850* (1930), p.85.) Such children were often dosed with opiates like Godfrey's Cordial to keep them quiet whilst the mother worked. But the earnings thus secured played a vital role in the family budget at a time when male labourers' wages were often abysmally low.

The variety of tasks which the women undertook is indicated by a report from Blything, Suffolk, early in the 1840s. Here, alongside seasonal work on farms, the women took on eight different kinds of 'domestic' employment. These comprised straw plaiting, knitting, tailoring, braiding herring nets for the local fishing trade, shoe-binding, making labourers' gloves for hedgecutting and the like, washing for wealthier members of the village community, and dressmaking. Similarly a report upon the counties of Wiltshire, Dorset, Devon and Somerset at this time noted:

> The kinds of agricultural labour in which women are engaged appear to depend upon the habits of narrow localities . . . it is nevertheless impossible to point out any very marked or essential difference between their employments in general in one county and in another. Thus working in the hay and corn harvests, or in the dairy; hoeing turnips; weeding and picking stones; planting and digging potatoes; pulling, digging, and hacking turnips; attending the threshing machine, and winnowing corn; beating manure; filling dung-carts; planting beans, &c., are common to all the counties, though by no means uniformly practised in every part of them; picking apples is confined to the cider counties; and leading horses at plough appears to be a practice of only a few and perhaps remote parts of Devonshire and Somersetshire. . . .
>
> The severest labour performed by women, connected with agriculture, is in the dairy-farms. The work lasts during the principal part of the year, and for many months occupies the greater part of the day. Milking and making cheese twice a-day, and at the same time looking after the cheese already made, are described to be 'work that is never finished.' . . . Dr. Greenup, of Calne, states, that he is not unfrequently applied to for advice by women suffering from symptoms of over-work, generally attributable to their being employed in the dairy, and that such symptoms are – pains in the back and limbs, overpowering sense of fatigue most painful in the morning, want of appetite, feverishness, &c. . . . .
>
> The wife and children also generally make some addition to the means of subsistence of the family by gleaning. . . . Five-and-twenty or thirty shillings

obtained in this way are an important item in the income of the family.

The earnings of the wife and children, from farm-labour, are common to all these counties; but in a considerable portion of Dorsetshire, and an equally large district of Devonshire, there are other occupations at which the wives and children of the farm-labourers gain as much or more than by being employed in agriculture. In the part of Dorsetshire in question, the shirt wire-button-making is followed by nearly all the labourers' wives and children, above six years old. The earnings of a family at button-making amount to 3s., 4s., 5s., and sometimes 6s., or even more, a-week. The importance of this employment to the family is perceptible in the unwillingness of the parents to let their children attend the schools where the work might be interrupted. . . . In the portion of Devonshire in question, lace-making occupies a great many of the daughters of the agricultural labourers from an early age, and their earnings are considerable. . . .

The clothing of women employed in field-labour would appear to be inadequate for their work, but the deficiency is not complained of by them. A change of clothes seems to be out of the question, although necessary not only for cleanliness but for convenience and saving of time. The upper parts of the underclothes of women at work, even their stays, quickly become wet through with perspiration, whilst the lower parts cannot escape getting equally wet in nearly every kind of work they are engaged in, except in the driest weather. It not unfrequently happens that a woman, on returning home from work, is obliged to go to bed for an hour or two to allow her clothes to be dried. It is also by no means uncommon for her, if she does not do this, to put them on again the next morning nearly as wet as when she took them off.

Reports of Special Assistant Poor Law Commissioners on the Employment of Women and Children in Agriculture, Parl. Papers (1843), Vol. XII, Report by Alfred Austin, pp.3-5; 16; 22.

But it is sadly true that for all their formidable labours – and ones which were essential for the welfare of their family – these field workers were little respected by better-off members of the rural community. The heavy manual labour they performed was thought to be degrading and they were widely condemned for their bad language. The Radical country clergyman and author, Charles Kingsley emphasised the low esteem in which they were held when his well-to-do hero, Lancelot, and the latter's gamekeeper visited a village feast day *incognito*:

> Lancelot had been already perfectly astonished at the foulness of language which prevailed; and the utter absence of anything like chivalrous respect, almost of common decency, towards women. But lo! the language of the elder women was quite as disgusting as that of the men, if not worse. He whispered a remark on the point to Tregarva, who shook his head.
>
> 'It's the field-work, sir – the field-work, that does it all. They get accustomed there from their childhood to hear words whose very meanings they shouldn't know; and the elder teach the younger ones, and the married ones are worst of all. It wears them out in body, sir, that field-work, and makes them brutes in soul and in manners.'
>
> 'Why don't they give it up? Why don't the respectable ones set their face against it?'
>
> 'They can't afford it, sir. They must go a-field, or go hungered, most of them. And they get to like the gossip, and scandal, and coarse fun of it, while their children are left at home to play in the roads, or fall into the fire, as plenty do every year.'
>
> 'Why not at school?'
>
> 'The big ones are kept at home, sir, to play at nursing those little ones who are too young to go. Oh, sir', he added, in a tone of deep feeling, 'it is very little of a father's care, or a mother's love, that a labourer's child knows in these days!'
>
> Charles Kingsley, *Yeast* (1848), pp.243-44.

Only with the improvement in farm workers' wages in the second half of the nineteenth century did the number of women workers on the land at last begin to fall sharply. Before that their earnings were too important a part of household income to be sacrificed.

Riots, Disturbances and the Punishment of Crime

Once the painful adjustment from war to peace had been accomplished a limited number of labouring families were able to enjoy a modest degree of comfort. Cobbett observed that farm workers in areas of forest and common land, where fuel was available and there was free grazing for livestock, were always better off than those in treeless arable districts. In November 1821 he commented approvingly of the Forest of Dean:

> The only good purpose that these forests answer is that of furnishing a place of being to labourers' families on their skirts; and here their cottages are very neat, and the people look hearty and well, just as they do round the forests in Hampshire. Every cottage has a pig, or two. These graze in the forest, and, in the fall, eat acorns and beech-nuts and the seed of the ash . . . . Some of these foresters keep cows, and all of them have bits of ground, cribbed, of course, at different times, from the forest: and to what better use can the ground be put? I saw several wheat stubbles from 40 rods to 10 rods. I asked one man how much wheat he had from about 10 rods. He said more than two bushels. Here is bread for three weeks, or more, perhaps; and a winter's straw for the pig besides. . . . The dead limbs and old roots of the forest give *fuel*; and how happy are these people, compared with the poor creatures about Great Bedwin and Cricklade, where they have neither land nor shelter, and where I saw the girls carrying home bean and wheat stubble for fuel!

William Cobbett, *Rural Rides*, Vol. I (1853), p.29.

A similar precarious security was enjoyed by the annually hired skilled workers on the farm, such as horsemen and shepherds, who were responsible for livestock care. Not only was their income assured, providing their employer stayed in business, for the period of their hiring, but it was the custom to provide many of them with rent-free cottages, as part of their contract. And although employers might impose restrictions upon their freedom of action within the home, at least they had a roof over their head. It was such a skilled worker's household that John Clare had in mind in the opening section of *The Shepherd's Calendar*:

> The shutter closd the lamp alight
> The faggot chopt and blazing bright
> The shepherd from his labour free
> Dancing his childern on his knee
> Or toasting sloe boughs sputtering ripe
> Or smoaking glad his puthering pipe
> While underneath his masters seat
> The tird dog lies in slumbers sweet
> Startling and whimpering in his sleep
> Chasing still the straying sheep
> The cat rolld round in vacant chair
> Or leaping childerns knees to lair
> Or purring on the warmer hearth
> Sweet chorus to the crickets mirth

> *   *   *

> Neath the yard hovel from the storm
> The swine well fed and in the sty
> And fowl snug perched in hovel nigh
> Wi head in feathers safe asleep

> *   *   *

> The huswife busy night and day
> Cleareth the supper things away
> While jumping cat starts from her seat

And streaking up on weary feet
The dog wakes at the welcome tones
That calls him up to pick the bones
On corner walls a glittering row
Hang fire irons less for use then show
Tongues bright wi huswifes rubbing toil
Whod sooner burn her hands then soil
When sticks want mending up

John Clare, *The Shepherd's Calendar* (1827),
ll.1-14; 30-35; 45-55.

Sadly, however, in much of southern and eastern England, where population growth had outstripped work-opportunities and there was high unemployment, labouring families experienced conditions very different from the cosy scene depicted by Clare. In the north, where coal was relatively cheap and alternative employment existed in manufacturing industry or the mines, the position was far easier. The men earned more and were spared 'that hopelessness which rotted village life in the southern counties'. It was during the winter that the anxieties of the southern labourers reached a peak. Any device which robbed them of work at that time was regarded with deep hostility, and paramount in this regard were mole ploughs for drainage work and threshing machines. During the Napoleonic Wars the latter had been deployed to counter labour shortages but they continued to be used in the post-war era too. Although the true reason for the labourers' distress lay in the large increase in the rural population, coupled with the general dislocations in arable agriculture at the time, threshing machines quickly became a convenient scapegoat for all ills. As early as 1815 there were reports of machine-breaking from Suffolk and this was extended on a far more serious scale in the following year to several parts of East Anglia. Eventually the unrest was suppressed with military help, and seven men involved in riots at Ely, Littleport and Downham Market were hanged. This draconian response by the authorities did not end the discontent, however, and sporadic outbursts recurred in 1822.

Such violence was indicative of the frustration felt by ill-paid and ill-fed men and women, for whom the future was bleak. They were forerunners of still larger uprisings which took place in the second half of 1830. These so-called 'Swing' riots occurred between August 1830 and January 1831 and were concentrated in the southern and south Midland counties. They followed a winter – 1829 – which had been particularly harsh and when low wages and unsympathetic treatment by parish poor law officials had fuelled the sense of bitterness in many communities.

The first move came at Lower Hardres near Canterbury on 28 August when a threshing machine was destroyed. The discontent reached its peak in the following November. But, as in the earlier disturbances, machine-breaking was only one aspect of the discontent. Barn and rick fires, the sending of threatening letters signed by the legendary 'Captain Swing', attacks on justices of the peace and parish overseers and demands for money and provisions all played their part. Rioting sometimes occurred in communities without threshing machines. In fact, the most significant feature seems to have been population size. A large village rioted, while a smaller one with the same grievances but less influence remained passive. Parishes in which Nonconformity was strong or where market and fairs provided centres for communication were more likely to protest than those without these characteristics. In some instances, too, politics played a role. There was excitement as news reached England of the overthrow of the monarchy in France for a second time and there were renewed campaigns for parliamentary reform in Britain itself. Radical newspapers also contributed, with Cobbett reporting in detail what he termed the 'rural war' in his *Political Register.* Although he condemned arson, he described graphically the misery which had provoked the risings and declared that but for the fires the 'military force . . . would long ago have subdued these half-starved machine-breakers'. To the government he seemed to be fomenting the trouble and in July 1831 he was unsuccessfully prosecuted for seditious libel. The strength of his language, which so aroused official ire, is exemplified in an article he wrote for the *Political Register* in December 1830:

All across the south, from Kent to Cornwall, and from Sussex to Lincolnshire, the commotion extends. . . .

The labourers of England see, at any rate, that the *thrashing-machines* rob them of the wages that they ought to receive. They, therefore, began by demolishing these machines. This was a *crime*; the magistrates and jailors were ready with punishments; soldiers, well fed and well clothed out of the taxes, were ready to shoot or cut down the offenders. Unable to resist these united forces, the labourers resorted to the use of *fire*, secretly put to the barns and stacks of those who had the machines, or whom they deemed the cause of their poverty and misery. The mischief and the alarm that they have caused by this means are beyond all calculation. They go in bands of from 100 to 1,000 men, and summon the farmers to come forth, and then they demand that they shall agree to pay them such wages as they think right; and you will please to observe, that even the wages that they demand are not so high by one-third as their grandfathers received, taking into consideration *the taxes* that they have now to pay. . . . The millions have, at last, broken forth; hunger has, at last, set stone walls at defiance, and braved the fetters and the gallows; nature has, at last, commanded the famishing man to get food. All the base and foolish endeavours to cause it to be believed that the fires are the work of *foreigners*, or of a *conspiracy*, or of *instigation* from others than labourers, only show that those who make these endeavours are conscious that they share, in some way or other, in the guilt of having been the real cause of the mischief.

William Cobbett, *Political Register*, 4 December 1830.

John Clare, writing anonymously in the Stamford *Champion* (11 January 1831), likewise mocked the official preoccupation with tracing the alleged inspirer of the uprising, the mythical Captain Swing, who seemed to move around the countryside with astonishing speed:

For some said his clothing was light, lack-a-day,
And some said his clothing was black,
Some saw him as two in a gig that was green;
Some as one on a horse that was black;
Today he sold matches and begged for a crust,
To keep a poor beggar alive,
To-morrow he scares all the dogs in the town,
Driving hard as the devil can drive,
While a day or two's wonder goes buzzing about,
Like a swarm of bees leaving a hive.

'The Hue and Cry', quoted in Roger Sales, *English
Literature in History, 1780-1830: Pastoral and Politics*
(1983), pp.101–102.

Yet, despite the drama of the disturbances, their incidence
was as variable as the scope of the issues with which they were
concerned. In Hampshire and Norfolk it was the destruction
of machinery that formed the prime objective of the rioters,
while in much of Sussex, Suffolk and Essex the protest was
against low wages. Again, while Kent, Hampshire and
Wiltshire were heavily involved, only about one Oxfordshire
parish in ten was affected. But to the propertied sectors of
society the unrest was sufficiently pervasive to create
widespread alarm. Military help was called upon, special
constables were sworn in, and eventually 1976 prisoners were
tried before 90 courts sitting in 34 counties. Of these, 19 were
hanged (all but 3 for arson), 481 were transported and over 600
more were imprisoned in this country.

Mary Russell Mitford, whose father was chairman of the
Reading bench of magistrates, witnessed the violence in her
area on the Berkshire/Hampshire border with mounting
anxiety. Something of the fear engendered in the 'respectable'
classes at the time is conveyed by her account of events.
Significantly she regarded the men involved as 'misguided', for
like many others at that time, she failed to recognise that they
had turned to violence only as a last desperate resort, out of
despair at the hopelessness of their situation:

No one that had the misfortune to reside during the
last winter in the disturbed districts of the south of

England, will ever forget the awful impression of that terrible time. The stilly gatherings of the misguided peasantry amongst the wild hills, partly heath and partly woodland, of which so much of the northern part of Hampshire is composed . . . or the open and noisy meetings of determined men at noontide in the streets and greens of our Berkshire villages, and even sometimes in the very churchyards, sallying forth in small but resolute numbers to collect money or destroy machinery, and compelling or persuading their fellow-labourers to join them at every farm they visited; or the sudden appearance and disappearance of these large bodies, who sometimes remained together to the amount of several hundreds for many days, and sometimes dispersed, one scarcely knew how, in a few hours; their day-light marches on the high road, regular and orderly as those of an army, or their midnight visits to lonely houses, lawless and terrific as the descent of pirates . . . all brought close to us a state of things which we never thought to have witnessed in peaceful and happy England. . . .

Nor were the preparations for defence, however necessary, less shocking than the apprehensions of attack. The hourly visits of bustling parish officers, bristling with importance (for our village, though in the centre of the insurgents, continued uncontaminated – 'faithful amidst the unfaithful found,' – and was, therefore, quite a rallying point for loyal men and true;) the swearing in of whole regiments of petty constables; the stationary watchmen, who every hour, to prove their vigilance, sent in some poor wretch, beggar or match-seller, or rambling child, under the denomination of suspicious persons; the mounted patrol, whose deep 'all's well,' which ought to have been consolatory, was about the most alarming of all alarming sounds; the soldiers, transported from place to place in carts the better to catch the rogues, whose local knowledge gave them great advantage in a dispersal; the grave processions of magistrates and gentlemen on horseback: and, above all, the nightly collecting of arms and armed men within our own dwelling, kept up a continual sense of nervous inquietude.

Fearful, however, as were the realities, the rumours were a hundred-fold more alarming. Not an hour passed but, from some quarter or other, reports came pouring in of mobs gathering, mobs assembled, mobs marching upon us. . . . So passed the short winter's day. With the approach of night came fresh sorrows; the red glow of fires gleaming on the horizon, and mounting into the middle sky; the tolling of bells; and the rumbling sound of the engines clattering along from place to place, and often, too often, rendered useless by the cutting of the pipes after they had begun to play – a dreadful aggravation of the calamity, since it proved that among those who assembled, professedly to help, were to be found favourers and abettors of the concealed incendiaries.

Mary Russell Mitford, *Our Village*, Vol. V (1832), pp.5-8.

Part of the law-and-order problem arose from the fact that at this time policing was still a very rudimentary affair, much as it had been in the eighteenth century. Largely it was left to a motley crew of parish constables and private prosecuting societies, reinforced occasionally by Bow Street runners sent down from London, or, after 1829, by metropolitan policemen. Much of the routine administration of the law was in the hands of magistrates, usually recruited from the landed gentry and the clergy, and carrying with them, inevitably, the prejudices of their class. Not until the end of the 1830s, almost a decade after the 'Swing' riots, did the position begin to change. In 1839/40 counties were at last allowed to acquire professional police forces under the new County Police Acts. But it was left to the County and Borough Police Act of 1856 to make the setting up of a county force obligatory. In the meantime, the confused state of policing arrangements, not merely in dealing with riots but with ordinary offences, such as robbery or burglary, was pinpointed in the report of the Royal

Commission on a Constabulary Force, issued in 1839. From one of the magistrates at Pershore, Worcestershire, came the following gloomy account:

> There is a great deal of crime (not heinous, perhaps) which is not brought to light, from the want of police, and the unwillingness, under such circumstances, of the injured to prosecute. The river Avon winds through the whole extent of the district (eighteen miles), and the number of barges employed upon it gives great facility to plunder in the night time, and to escape detection, many of the bargemen being of the worst character. Since the magistrates have been engaged in answering these queries the skin and entrails of a fresh-killed sheep were taken out of the river in an eel-net close to the town of Pershore, and although notice has been sent to all the neighbouring farmers, not one will own to having lost a sheep, for fear of being obliged to prosecute. They call it 'throwing away good money after bad'. If reluctance to prosecute prevailed so much before, it has now been strengthened in this neighbourhood by the late Act of Parliament allowing counsel to prisoners. Mr. Tidmarsh, a large farmer, having at different times lost four fat sheep, succeeded at last in discovering the offenders, and the evidence was so strong against two persons charged, that they made a confession before the committing magistrate, and implored the mercy of the prosecutor. The ingenuity of counsel, however, at the last quarter sessions prevailed, and the prisoners were acquitted. The farmers say, 'After this, what use is there in prosecuting?'
>
> *Report of Royal Commission on a Constabulary Force*, Parl. Papers (1839), Vol. XIX, p.5.

Their counterparts at Droitwich, Worcestershire, noted the role of vagrants in the commission of crime: 'There are reasons to believe that the burglaries, horse-stealing, and cattle-stealing, whenever they occur, are committed by strangers; –

that the burglars are supposed to come from Birmingham; the horse-stealers still farther off. The sheep-stealer is generally a labourer resident in the parish where the offence is committed, or of an adjoining parish, and rarely escapes detection. Again, the cottager's dwelling is in the daytime frequently broken into by trampers and others in the guise of seafaring men, whilst the inmates are at labour in the field.' And although mounted highwaymen no longer patrolled the nation's roads, robberies by footpads were still quite common. 'When the farmers had occasion to return from the market,' said one East Anglian witness, 'they made their arrangements to go home two, or three, or four together. One robbery committed in a district will create . . . remarkable alarm all through that district' (Ibid, p.89). It was this lawless situation that the professional police forces were designed to combat.

For those caught, as the 'Swing' riots demonstrated, the penalties imposed could be severe, with death or transportation available for a whole range of crimes, varying from the trivial to the serious. By 1820 there were no less than 200 capital offences. Poaching was particularly heavily punished (see Chapter 4, pp.137-43). Horse, sheep and cattle stealing, too, remained capital crimes until 1832, while for 20 years after that date they could be punished by transportation. Yet, as with many other offences, the fate of men convicted could in practice vary widely. Whilst one sheep-stealer was hanged, another, perhaps with a better reputation or more influential friends, would be imprisoned for a few months only. Of 288 persons found guilty of this offence between 1823-25 4 were executed, 148 transported for life, 32 transported for 14 years and, at the other extreme, 10 were imprisoned for 6 months or less. Uncertainty of sentence, according to the attitude of magistrates and the judiciary, remained an unhappy feature of the legal system throughout the period.

The Relief of the Poor

If the 'Swing' riots of 1830 had focused attention upon the question of law and order, they also aroused interest in the poor-relief system. This was not a new phenomenon. As early as the 1780s George Crabbe had stressed the misery of those forced to accept the doubtful protection of the parish poorhouse:

> Theirs is yon house that holds the parish poor,
> Whose walls of mud scarce bear the broken door;
> There, where the putrid vapours, flagging, play,
> And the dull wheel hums doleful through the day –
> There children dwell, who know no parents' care;
> Parents, who know no children's love, dwell there!
> Heart-broken matrons on their joyless bed,
> Forsaken wives, and mothers never wed;
> Dejected widows with unheeded tears,
> And crippled age with more than childhood fears;
> The lame, the blind, and, far the happiest they!
> The moping idiot and the madman gay.
> Here too the sick their final doom receive,
> Here brought, amid the scenes of grief, to grieve,
>
>   *   *   *
>
> Here, on a matted flock, with dust o'erspread,
> The drooping wretch reclines his languid head;
> For him no hand the cordial cup applies,
> Or wipes the tear that stagnates in his eyes;
> No friends with soft discourse his pain beguile,
> Or promise hope till sickness wears a smile.

> George Crabbe, *The Village* (1783), Book I,
> ll.228-41; 268-73.

But the sense of discontent and bitterness in 1830 was different. Not only was hatred of the Poor Law an explicit feature of many of the 'Swing' disturbances, with parish overseers singled out for attack in a number of parishes, but often it appeared that the worst riots had occurred in places where relief payments were at their highest. It could, of course, be argued that it was precisely in those districts that unemployment and social deprivation were also at a peak and labourers' desperation consequently most acute, but in official circles the coincidence reinforced dissatisfaction with the way the relief system had evolved since 1815. In 1817 and 1819 national expenditure on poor relief had reached a peak of almost £8 million per annum, compared to less than £2 million a year so spent in 1783-85; and although the figure then fell back, the amount expended remained significant. In 1831 alone it amounted to around £7 million.

From the propertied classes came allegations that receipt of relief was no longer regarded as a stigma by labouring men, and that their desire to find independent employment was undermined by the parish aid available. In these circumstances a Royal Commission on the Poor Laws was appointed in 1832 and from its pages information can be gleaned of the kind of system – or lack of it – which had developed. Inevitably its accounts were biased in that it was *looking* for points to criticise. But, equally, there is little doubt that the 'facts' it presented were accurate. Thus at Swallowfield in Berkshire, and a number of other parishes both in that county and elsewhere, it was customary to 'make up' wages out of the poor rates to what was considered an adequate sum, bearing in mind the price of bread and the size of a man's family. 'The bread money is hardly looked upon by the labourers in the light of parish relief,' the Report declared. 'They consider it as much their right as the wages they receive from their employers, and in their own minds make a wide distinction between "taking their bread money" and "going on the parish".' (*The Poor Law Report of 1834*, eds S.G. and E.O.A. Checkland (1974) p. 98.) The 'bread scale' policy had been initiated by magistrates meeting at Speenhamland in Berkshire during 1795, as a response to the sharp rise in food prices. But it was soon adopted in a number of adjoining counties, and in the following year was approved by parliament. Only in the north of England, where competing employment in manufacturing and mining kept wages high, did such devices prove unnecessary.

Another arrangement was the 'roundsman' system, under which the unemployed were sent from one ratepayer to another until they found someone willing to engage them, at a wage subsidised by the parish. Not surprisingly, the workers concerned had little interest in the tasks they undertook as 'roundsmen', since they were given relief whether they performed well or not.

> In other cases the parish contracts with some individual to have some work performed for him by the paupers at a given price, the parish paying the paupers. In many places the roundsman system is effected by means of an auction. Mr. Richardson states that in Sulgrave, Northamptonshire, the old and infirm are sold at the monthly meeting to the best bidder, at prices varying, according to the time of the year from 1s. 6d. a week to 3s.; that at Yardley Hastings, all the unemployed men are put up to sale weekly, and that the clergyman of the parish told him that he had seen ten men the last week knocked down to one of the farmers for 5s. and that there were at that time about seventy men let out in this manner out of a body of 170.

> S.G. and E.O.A. Checkland (eds), *The Poor Law Report of 1834*, pp.102–103.

Elsewhere other variants applied. At Pollington, Yorkshire,

> they send many of them upon the highways, but they only work four hours per day; this is because there is not employment sufficient in that way; they sleep more than they work, and if any but the surveyor found them sleeping, they would laugh at them. ... At Deddington, [Oxfordshire] during the severe winter months, about sixty men apply every morning to the overseer for work or pay. He ranges them, under a shed in a yard. If a farmer or any one else wants a man, he sends to the yard for one, and pays half the day's wages; the rest is paid by the parish. At the close of the day the unemployed are paid the wages of a day, minus 2d.'

> Ibid, pp.109; 112.

And so the catalogue went on. Not surprisingly, when the commission's report appeared in 1834, it led to immediate demands for widespread reform. The 1834 Poor Law

Amendment Act was designed to that end. Henceforward a Central Board was to oversee the whole poor law system, while at local level out-relief, save for medical attention, was to be ended for the able-bodied. Instead they were to receive indoor aid only, within a workhouse, with paupers classified and separated according to age and sex and with families divided. The prime objective was to make the pauper's position 'less eligible', that is more unpleasant, than that of any independent labourer and thereby to discourage applications for assistance. But in the long run, indoor relief proved more expensive than outdoor payments, so these were continued in many areas, albeit at a minimal level. The 'less eligibility' aspect was retained, however, and among the poor there grew up a bitter hatred of the bureaucratic, unsympathetic regime introduced by the new Poor Law authorities, or unions, as they were called. Each was made up of a group of about fifteen to thirty neighbouring parishes, with elected guardians to act as administrators.

Among the landed classes, meanwhile, there were those unfeeling enthusiasts like Lord Everingham in Benjamin Disraeli's *Coningsby* (1844) who 'looked upon the New Poor-law as another Magna Charta'. Or Lord Marney who firmly proclaimed that it

> would be the salvation of the country, provided it was "carried out" in the spirit in which it was developed in the Marney Union; . . . . We continue reducing the rates, and as long as we do that the country must improve. The workhouse test tells. We had the other day a case of incendiarism, which frightened some people; but I inquired into it, and am quite satisfied it originated in purely accidental circumstances; at least nothing to do with wages. . . . Nothing can put this country right but emigration on a great scale; and as the Government do not choose to undertake it, I have commenced it for my own defence on a small scale. I will take care that the population of my parishes is not increased. I build no cottages, and I destroy all I can; and I am not ashamed or afraid to say so.

> Benjamin Disraeli, *Sybil* (1845), pp.54; 112-13.

Disraeli himself, as a leading member of the 'Young England' wing of the Tory party, was a strong opponent of the 1834 legislation, introduced by a Whig government. He condemned the substitution of centralised relief for the old system based on local administration and paternalistic principles. In his novels these hostile political attitudes inevitably showed through in his unsympathetic portraits of grandees like Lord Marney and Lord Everingham.

A very different approach from theirs was expressed by another member of landed society, old Mrs Buckhurst:

> not all the candour I can school myself into expressing, can avail to make me approve the erection of that bare-faced monster of a Union Poor-house, which seems to glare upon us with its hundred eyes from what used to be the prettiest meadow in the parish. I wish I had not seen, the only time I ever ventured near enough to look at it, . . . old Simon Rose, with his granddaughter, poor soul! and her three little ones, standing before that dreadful Richard Dempster, the governor, looking as if they thought that life and death depended on his will. I have never got the group out of my head since. All the fearful change in the treatment of the poor, which has followed the erection of this prison-like place, *may* be very useful. I am too old to dare express a doubt upon the subject . . . . But even the new commissioner himself might be inclined to make some allowance for the poor blundering old people of the district, if he did but know the contrast between what they see now and what they looked on formerly. We gave a worse name to our house of refuge there . . . than the new folks have given theirs. We called it the workhouse, which bears a sort of threatening in its very name; and it was not, nor was it intended to be, a dwelling to be desired or sought for. But oh! the heavy change! Deepbrook Workhouse was to Deepbrook Union what a free state is to a slave state in America . . . .
>
> Frances Trollope, *Jessie Phillips* (1844), p.16.

For their part the rural poor shared these apprehensions. Thomas Hood in *The Lay of the Labourer* stressed the lengths to which a man would go to keep himself and his family from 'the house':

> Wherever Nature needs
> Wherever Labour calls,
> No job I'll shirk of the hardest work,
> To shun the workhouse walls;
> Where savage laws begrudge
> The pauper babe its breath,
> And doom a wife to a widow's life,
> Before her partner's death.

> ✻   ✻   ✻

> No parish money, or loaf,
> No pauper badges for me,
> A son of the soil, by right of toil
> Entitled to my fee.
> No alms I ask, give me my task:
> Here are the arm, the leg,
> The strength, the sinews of a Man,
> To work, and not to beg.

Thomas Hood, *The Lay of the Labourer*, ll.51-58;
67-74.

To some paupers even jail became preferable to the union house, or the 'bastille', as they nicknamed it. From Suffolk in about 1850 it was reported:

> The manner in which the provisions of the law were put into execution during the early period of its operation, . . . [was] in direct opposition to the dictates of humanity, and in some cases exceeded the provisions of the Act itself. In several unions out-door relief was almost entirely abolished, and in-door relief was made nearly as unbearable as any civilised community, boasting of a haven of mercy in its bosom, could

permit; and the positive dread and horror in which the workhouses were in consequence held, the want of kindly feeling too frequently manifested by officials, and the cutting asunder of family ties, tended to make our poor not only abhor the union-house, but has often induced them to seek the shelter of the prison instead . . . .

In the Eleventh Report of the Inspectors of Prisons it is stated that one of the prisoners in the Ipswich County Gaol said, 'They wanted me to go into the Union, but I would rather go to the Gaol than the House.' Another stated, 'The Union and the Gaol are one – both prisons; the Union a worse prison than this.'

John Glyde, Jr, *Suffolk in the Nineteenth Century*
(1856), pp.183-86.

Thanks to these stringent policies, national poor-rate expenditure fell from £7 million in 1831 to between £4.5 million and £5 million per annum in the decade following the passage of the 1834 Poor Law Amendment Act, while for twenty years after that, it fluctuated between £5 million and £6 million a year. But if the curbing of poor relief expenditure was a continuing object of the system, in other ways a relaxation of attitudes slowly became apparent. Although many poor-law guardians shared the unsympathetic stance of Lord Marney, others saw it as part of their duty to ensure that the poor received fair treatment. In January 1838 Greville wrote in his diary of the Duke of Rutland:

The Duke . . . is as selfish a man as any of his class – that is, He never does what he does not like, and spends his whole life in a round of such pleasures as suit his taste, but he is neither a foolish nor a bad man, and partly from a sense of duty, and partly from inclination, he devotes time and labour to the interest and welfare of the people who live and labour on his estate. He is a Guardian of a very large Union, and he not only attends regularly the meetings of Poor Law Guardians every week or fortnight, and takes an active part in their proceedings, but he visits those paupers who receive out-of-doors relief, sits and converses with them, invites them to complain to him if they have anything to complain of, and tells them that he is not only their friend but their representative at the Assembly of Guardians, and that it is his duty to see that they are nourished and protected. To my mind there is more 'sympathy' in this than in railing at the rich and rendering the poor discontented . . . .

> Lytton Strachey and Roger Fulford (eds), *The Greville Memoirs* (1938), Vol. IV, p.9.

Political Affairs

The changes inaugurated in poor law administration and policing during the 1830s and beyond symbolised the rise of the professional administrator at the expense of the amateur. Inevitably this growing professionalism reduced the role of the landed classes and the magistracy, although until the 1880s the change was not radical. County government throughout the period remained largely in the hands of the landowners and clergy, many of whom came from landed families. They also became committee members of hospital boards and similar bodies in their area and frequently took the chair at meetings of local societies or at official dinners. All of this reinforced their status within the community.

On the national political scene a comparable degree of control was retained. Not only was the position of the landed interest supreme within the House of Lords, but it dominated the Commons as well:

> The English aristocracy [declared a German visitor in 1828] has indeed the most solid advantages over those of all other countries – from its real wealth, and yet more from the share in the legislative power allotted to it by the Constitution: *but . . . it is not upon these grounds that it chooses to assert or to justify its supremacy, but precisely upon its assumed noble blood*

and higher extraction . . . . The spirit of *caste*, which, emanating from this source, descends through all stages of society in greater or less force, has received here a power, consistency and full development, wholly unexampled in any other country.

E.M. Butler (ed.), *A Regency Visitor: The English Tour of Prince Pückler-Muskau, 1826-1828*, pp.333-34.

Even the passage of the 1832 Reform Act, enfranchising some of the new industrial towns, made little change to the overall balance of political power and it was not until 1885 that commercial men and manufacturers outnumbered landowners in the Commons. Often, as in Disraeli's *Coningsby* or Trollope's *Framley Parsonage*, leading political figures would meet at one or other of the large country houses to discuss party tactics and to plan for the future. 'England is unrivalled for two things, sporting and politics', wrote Disraeli in 1844. 'They were combined at Beaumanoir; for the guests came not merely to slaughter the Duke's pheasants, but to hold council on the prospects of the party'. (Benjamin Disraeli, *Coningsby*, Book II, p.91.)

At constituency level it was accepted that in agricultural districts 'tenants voted with their landlords, and it was a binding convention of electioneering to write to the principal landowners soliciting the support of their interest, just as it was considered only prudent and polite to ask the permission of a landlord before canvassing his tenants'. (F.M.L. Thompson, *English Landed Society in the Nineteenth Century* (1963), p.200.) Electoral corruption persisted, since the Reform Act neither imposed a maximum for official expenses nor laid down any effective measure against bribery. The £14 000 needed to contest the South Durham seat in 1843 was, in Lord Harry Vane's view, 'scandalously preposterous', almost enough to cause his retirement from active politics. But it was not unique. Most electors seem to have regarded the right to vote as a useful piece of property to be bargained away in exchange for a lower rental for their farms or a generous payment in cash or kind at the appropriate time.

In some respects the Reform Act even strengthened the hold of the large landowners over the county constituencies, since it enfranchised new categories of leaseholders, copyholders and tenant farmers, who were vulnerable to pressure from a landlord or his agent to vote in the way they desired. At the 1837 General Election Earl Cawdor's agent in Carmarthen wrote to the tenants firmly informing them: 'I shall depend upon you to plump for Colonel Trevor at the coming election, who is the only candidate supported by your noble landlord, and I have no doubt that you will do so'. He also instructed a sub-agent to interview four tenants who were suspected of wishing to support the other side and who were in arrears with their rent, pointing out that if they were to show themselves so ungrateful to their landlord, they must pay their rents immediately and he would then see 'what further is to be done in the matter'. Again, on the Netherby estate in Cumberland, Sir James Graham's agent persuaded his employer to strengthen his forces in the county in the mid-1830s by creating extra votes on the estate through the use of joint tenancies. Only so, he argued, could the landed interest avoid 'being swamped by the too preponderating strength of the Towns'.

But in the main the influence of the principal landholders was preserved by less obvious strategems. Thus the Duke of Omnium

> was a Whig who gave very little practical support to any set of men, and very little practical opposition to any other set. He was above troubling himself with such sublunar matters. At election time he supported, and always carried, Whig candidates: and in return he had been appointed lord lieutenant of the county by one Whig minister, and had received the Garter from another. But these things were matters of course to a Duke of Omnium. He was born to be a lord lieutenant and a Knight of the Garter.
>
> Anthony Trollope, *Framley Parsonage* (1860), p.84.

Partly that self-confident attitude was a product of the landlord's belief that his leadership should be accepted unquestioningly by tenants and other social subordinates because his special position gave him the ability to judge in the interests of all, but partly it represented a residual survival of the old view that a bond of unity and loyalty should link all those who lived on the same estate. Both concepts were clearly to the fore in a letter written by a Northumbrian squire, Sir Charles Monck, to tenants on his north Lincolnshire estate in 1852:

> Nothing is more agreeable to the Constitution, and to all ancient usages of the Kingdom, or more advantageous to true liberty, than that landlords should endeavour by all fair means to lead their tenants. The Queen leads the Nation, and landlords in a similar manner lead their tenants. But there is a common interest between the Queen and the nation: so also between landlords and their tenants . . . . I expect of my tenants that they shall not engage their votes before they have communicated with me and come to know my wishes . . . . If it shall after that appear that my wishes and yours are in contrarity there then ought to be the fullest explanation and consideration between us . . . . I promise you that to the opinion of the majority I will submit. But . . . if I am bound to set an example of submission to the majority, the minority must be bound to follow that example, that the estate might not be divided, but act with its full weight for the benefit of all.
>
> Quoted in R.J. Olney, *Lincolnshire Politics 1832-1885* (1973), p.35.

In the event, the tenants consulted with each other and decided to support the candidate of Monck's choice. But they also pointed out that as they expected 'a continuation of low prices, . . . it will require our best energy and economy in the management of our farms aided by your kind assistance in competing with the produce of other countries who are less burdened with taxation than ourselves'. Monck received their letter with satisfaction and expressed his willingness 'to have the rents of the estate fixed so that both you and I shall have just share in the profits of active, skilful and commercial cultivation'. It was a neat example of mutual political bargaining.

One who saw the post-Reform electoral system in operation from the 'inside' was John Buckmaster, a former farm labourer from Slapton, Buckinghamshire. He became associated with the Anti-Corn Law League, a pressure group backed by urban industrial interests, whose objective was the repeal of the Corn Laws. His account of an election at 'Arlingford', as he named the country town constituency in question, showed clearly the persistence of dubious electoral practices after 1832, including heavy expenditure on alcohol. The contest took place in the early 1840s and involved a Tory pro-Protection candidate – nicknamed the Farmers' Friend – and a Free Trader.

> In manufacturing districts elections were comparatively safe and easy, but in small agricultural boroughs, where farmers spent their money with tradespeople, and one or two lawyers had managed to get the affairs of the corporation into their hands, the contest was by no means easy or certain. The struggle went on for weeks, and during that time there was little or no business, except at the public-houses, and as the final day drew near the excitement increased. Every public-house window had a placard, 'The committee sit here daily.' Then there was a liberal circulation of electioneering literature on both sides, sometimes personal and scurrilous. The central committee, which often consisted of a man and a boy, was besieged from morning to night with a seedy, dilapidated, red-nosed lot of fellows who wanted to be employed as canvassers, runners, clerks, scouts, messengers, watchers, and poets. . . .
>
> The constituency of Arlingford was about three hundred. The candidates had issued their addresses, and it was some days before they appeared before the free and independent electors. The Farmers' Friend was a feeble lot. He talked about the Constitution, Church, and State, protection to native industry, and something

about the Malt tax, but his lack of oratory was made up by the most boisterous manifestations of applause from his supporters, who cheered and hurrahed every word. Our candidate was a good speaker, and he made an excellent impression on the non-electors and some of the more thoughtful electors who were free to vote. Speechifying, drinking, bill-sticking, and canvassing were in full swing; and from the canvassing books – for, against, neutral, doubtful – there appeared some chance at least of a close contest. Put not your trust in canvassing books! The men canvassing on both sides used to meet at a public-house and arrange their books. The only trustworthy canvass was that voluntarily made by the candidates and their friends a few days before the election . . . .

The show of hands was in favour of the Free Trader, and for a few hours our candidate was member for Arlingford. The polling next day reversed the decision . . . . The poll was declared every hour, and for the first few hours we had a small majority. At one o'clock we were six behind, and at four we lost by twenty-three. The Tory Farmers' Friend was returned! The Free Trader and most of his friends left before the close of the poll. I remained behind with a clerk for a few days to settle the accounts. Nearly five weeks had been occupied in swearing, lying, drinking, fighting, and speechifying, and during this time much sin and wickedness of a worst (*sic*) kind was committed. Law-suits between relations and friends sprang up, and hatred in many cases became permanent. The streets still rang with 'Rule Britannia' and 'God save the Queen,' . . . . The chairing of the member was the last act in the pantomime of a free and independent election.

John Buckmaster, *A Village Politician* (1897), pp.195-201.

Buckmaster's natural chagrin apart, there is no doubt that pressure was exerted upon electors by those with power and patronage in order to persuade them to vote in the way required. These problems persisted to varying degrees as long as open voting survived, that is, until the passage of the Secret Ballot Act of 1872. Only in the 1840s, over the issue of the Corn Laws, did some farmers break with convention and display independent views opposed to the wishes of their free-trade landlord.

The 1840s saw an undermining of Protectionist food policies both as a result of changing economic conditions within Britain as a whole, and in the face of the powerful agitation of the Anti-Corn Law League. It culminated in the Repeal of the Corn Laws in 1846, an action which split the Conservative party and opened the British market to foreign grain supplies on a virtually unrestricted scale. Many farmers and a number of the smaller squires regarded the Tory Prime Minister, Sir Robert Peel, and his supporters as traitors who had betrayed earlier promises by this change of policy. In some cases this led to their nominating their own Protectionist candidates for election to parliament against the candidate of a Free Trade larger landowner. At the 1852 general election the County Farmers' Association in Cambridgeshire helped to elect a Protectionist and a similar success was recorded in Berkshire. Elsewhere pressure groups were formed in an unsuccessful attempt to overturn Peel's policy and old party alignments were thrown into confusion, as with Anthony Trollope's fictional squire of Ullathorne:

> In politics, Mr. Thorne was an unflinching conservative. . . . When that terrible crisis of free trade had arrived, when the repeal of the corn laws was carried by those very men whom Mr. Thorne had hitherto regarded as the only possible saviours of his country, he was for a time paralysed. His country was lost; but that was comparatively a small thing. Other countries had flourished and fallen, and the human race still went on improving under God's providence. But now all trust in human faith must for ever be at an end. Not only must ruin come, but it must come through the apostasy of those who had been regarded as the truest of true believers. Politics in England, as a pursuit for gentlemen, must be at an end. Had Mr. Thorne been

1. The drawing room of a well-to-do eighteenth century landed family by John Harden. Mother and daughters are occupying themselves by reading and writing.

2. *Reapers*, an engraving by George Stubbs, 1791. Even the womenfolk were expected to lend a hand with the harvest, which was the focal point of the farming year.

3. *Labourers*, as employed on Lord Torrington's estate at Southill, from an engraving by George Stubbs, 1789.

4. Machine-breaking and the firing of ricks were two of the most frightening aspects of the 'Swing' riots.

WE the undersigned Magistrates acting in and for the Hundred of Gallow, in the County of Norfolk, do promise to use our utmost Endeavours and Influence we may possess, to prevail upon the Occupiers of Land in the said Hundred,

To discontinue the use of Thrashing Machines, and to take them to pieces.

Dated this 29th. day of November, 1830.

CHAS. TOWNSHEND.
ROBERT NORRIS.
EDW. MARSHAM.

STEWARDSON AND SON, PRINTERS, FAKENHAM

5. The 'Swing' riots of 1830.

6. Children employed in a mid-nineteenth century agricultural gang in the Eastern Counties. For some of the over-worked and ill-fed youngsters the task proved too much.

trodden under foot by a Whig, he could have borne it as a Tory and a martyr; but to be so utterly thrown over and deceived by those he had so earnestly supported, so thoroughly trusted, was more than he could endure and live. He therefore ceased to live as a politician, and refused to hold any converse with the world at large on the state of the country.

Such were Mr. Thorne's impressions for the first two or three years after Sir Robert Peel's apostasy; but by degrees his temper, as did that of others, cooled down. He began once more to move about, to frequent the bench and the market, and to be seen at dinners, shoulder to shoulder with some of those who had so cruelly betrayed him. ... He, however, and others around him who still maintained the same staunch principles of protection – men like himself, who were too true to flinch at the cry of a mob – had their own way of consoling themselves. They were, and felt themselves to be, the only true depositaries left of certain Eleusinian mysteries, of certain deep and wondrous services of worship by which alone the gods could be rightly approached.

Anthony Trollope, *Barchester Towers* (1857),
p.194.

The Duke of Richmond, one of the national leaders of the Protectionist cause, underlined the bitter feelings aroused by these events when he angrily observed:

in 1841 the tenant-farmers of the country returned their representatives to Parliament for the great object of maintaining protection to themselves as growers of corn, and to the other branches of domestic industry. They could not blame the farmers because some of these representatives had either been seduced or converted to hold other views than those for which they had been elected: in which class these men were to be put, they would have an opportunity of judging when the time arrived for giving them the reward which they were to receive for their change of opinions; but in the mean time it was a great hardship to the tenant-farmer, who had expended a large amount of capital in the improvement of the farm he had taken for 19 or 30 years on the faith of protection, and that his rent was to be paid with the price of wheat at from 50s. to 56s. a quarter – it was a great hardship to make that tenant adhere to his lease when wheat came down to 40s. a quarter. . . . The farmers were an open-hearted, unsuspicious race of men, and they never expected that the House of Lords would turn round like a weathercock and change their opinions at the beck of any Minister, be he who he might. He thought that Sir Robert Peel could never be justified, in the eyes of any body of men, for the conduct he had pursued.

Hansard, 3rd Series, Vol. 87 (19 June 1846), cols 669-84 *passim*. Debate on the Corn Importation Bill.

Even Earl Fitzwilliam, a long-standing Free Trader, who considered the Corn Laws an ineffective means of protecting farmers, was doubtful about the way the policy had been implemented. He shared the view of his friend and fellow landowner, Evelyn Denison, that it had seemed to 'put the trading interest in ascendancy over the landed'.

Not until the mid-1850s, when Peel himself was dead and there was a resurgence of agricultural prosperity, after the uncertainties of the post-Repeal years, were the political wounds of the dispute healed. And the Squire Thornes of this world were able once more to move freely and comfortably among those whom they had regarded as their betrayers.

Occasional conflicts between individual landowners over electoral matters were, of course, not new. As early as 1838 William Howitt had referred to the 'uproar and exasperation' which a county election could engender among the higher ranks of rural society: 'when it does come to the country Hall, it comes, often as a hurricane, and frequently shakes it to the foundation, leaving in its track, debts and mortgages, shyness between neighbours, and rancour amongst old friends'. (William Howitt, *The Rural Life of England* (1838), Vol. I, p.108.) But the split of the 1840s was more ominous. It signalled to the landed classes that their political and economic power was on the wane in the face of the rising influence of urban industrialism and commerce. Although the reality of that changing situation was disguised for more than a decade, by the late 1860s and beyond the signs had become unmistakable.

4 The Rural Community

At the mansion-house at Kington is a fish-pond, well stocked with carp, eels, tench, &c. Many of these I have taken with rod and line, and others by fastening hooks with worms at the ends of pieces of string, and leaving them during the night. . . . Another amusement, and trespass, legally called poaching, I was taught in early life to pursue; by fixing wires, with nooses, in the holes of hedges, where hares and rabbits had beaten tracks. These sports arose from idleness, – from want of good companions, – from the absence of all moral and legal authority in the parish. Without a regular clergyman to advise and admonish, or a magistrate, or private gentleman residing in the principal house of the village, the inhabitants were undisciplined, illiterate, and deprived of all good example . . . .

> *The Autobiography of John Britton* (1850), p.29.
> (Britton was born at Kington, Wiltshire in 1771.)

You are sensible . . . that any amusement . . . must depend upon times and seasons. We are a very absurd nation . . . . Do but recollect these last ten years. The beginning of October, one is certain that everybody will be at Newmarket, and the Duke of Cumberland will lose, and Shafto [*an MP and enthusiastic gambler on horses*] win, two or three thousand pounds . . . . November passes, with two or three self-murders, and a new play. Christmas arrives; everybody goes out of town; and a riot happens in one of the theatres.

> Horace Walpole to Lord Hertford, 29 December 1763, in *Horace Walpole's Correspondence*, Vol. 38, pp.272-73.

Community Relationships

As John Britton's quotation indicates, it was considered the duty of the clergy and leading landed families in Georgian and early Victorian England to provide guidance and moral instruction to members of the lower orders living within their parishes. But, as he also shows, many villages lacked both of these sources of influence. Even the incumbent might be non-resident, at a time when plurality of livings was common, and the greater part of parochial work would thus devolve upon an ill-paid curate.

Yet, well into the nineteenth century, attachment to the local community remained a major feature of the day-to-day life of most country people. Even migration to seek fresh employment rarely extended beyond a ten-mile radius from a worker's place of origin. The growth of population in the northern industrial counties took place not by dramatic long-distance movements of large numbers of people, but by a series of short migrations, as well as by the above-average birth rate in many of those areas. Allied to this, there were strong kinship ties with much intermarrying within a relatively limited geographical area, while outsiders, especially in the more remote communities, were regarded with suspicion. Colonel John Byng, visiting the Isle of Portland in the late summer of 1782, noted that there was widespread inter-marrying among the inhabitants because they dreaded the 'alliance of foreigners'. Elsewhere it was not uncommon for villagers to turn out and stone a wayfarer for no other reason than that he was a stranger. In George Eliot's *Silas Marner* much of the suspicion which the linen weaver aroused was due to the fact that he was an 'outsider': 'No one knew where wandering men had their homes or their origin; and how was a man to be explained unless you at least knew somebody who knew his father and mother? To the peasants of old times, the world outside their own direct experience was a region of vagueness and mystery'. (George Eliot, *Silas Marner* (1861), p.4.)

Poor communications were a major factor in this survival of localism, with villagers thrown upon their own resources both for help in adversity and for entertainment during their leisure hours. John Britton stressed the isolation of Kington in the later eighteenth century:

> Though the street (if it may be so called) was a public road, it was rarely traversed by a post-chaise, or private carriage; a strange cart, or waggon, was seldom seen; and a stage-coach, then called a 'diligence,' never. Carriages of the last-mentioned kind were indeed scarcely known to the villagers; as only two or three passed through the neighbouring town of Chippenham on their way between Bath, Bristol, and London. . . . There were ten agriculturists who kept horses, cows, and sheep, and about the same number of tradesmen, or 'dealers and chapmen;' but I do not think there was a newspaper or magazine purchased by one of the inhabitants before the year 1780, when the London riots were talked about, and wondered at. . . . One of the Bath papers was afterwards introduced to the village, and created an epoch, – food for the gossip of the whole village . . . .
>
> [An] occasional visitant to the grassy street of the village, was a *Mountebank Doctor*, with his *Merry-Andrew* and stage caravan, or carriage. This itinerant quack was, however, a rare guest at our poor place; for the repetition of his visits to any town or village was regulated by the amount of shillings he could abstract from the pockets of his admiring auditors. . . .
>
> During the winter season, the drowsy monotony of 'Our Village' was occasionally awakened from its lethargy by the musical and stimulating cry of the Duke of Beaufort's fox-hounds, or by Sir James Tylney Long's harriers.
>
> *The Autobiography of John Britton* (1850),
> pp.27-34.

Even among the better-off members of rural society during the earlier part of the period visits to London or the larger provincial centres remained relatively rare, save for those with a power-base in national politics or at court. Mrs Hardcastle's plaintive appeals to her husband for greater variety in their daily round were doubtless echoes by other wives of small country squires:

> I vow, Mr. Hardcastle, you're very particular. Is there a creature in the whole country, but ourselves, that does not take a trip to town now and then, to rub off the rust a little? There's the two Miss Hoggs, and our neighbour, Mrs. Grigsby, go to take a month's polishing every winter. . . . Here we live in an old rumbling mansion, that looks for all the world like an inn, but that we never see company. Our best visitors are old Mrs. Oddfish, the curate's wife, and little Cripplegate, the lame dancing-master: And all our entertainment your old stories of Prince Eugene and the Duke of Marlborough. I hate such old-fashioned trumpery.

> Oliver Goldsmith, *She Stoops to Conquer* (1773), I.i.

Later, as roads and coaching facilities improved, the desire for more sophisticated urban amusements became easier to gratify, although in some quarters the seasonal flitting from the countryside which resulted was condemned as a dereliction of duty on the part of the landed families involved. R.S. Surtees, writing in the mid-1830s, drew favourable attention to Mr Farquharson of Langton House, near Blandford, Dorset, who not only financed the local hunt out of his own pocket but spent most of his time upon his estate: 'without flattery, I think Mr. Farquharson may be held up as a model of his order', Surtees declared. 'He resides nearly the whole year on his estate, spending his large income in the county whence he draws it, promoting the amusement of his friends and neighbours and discharging all the public duties that pertain to his position'. (E.D. Cuming, ed., *Town and Country Papers by Robert Smith Surtees* (1929), p.127.) Forty years earlier Colonel John Byng had made a similar point when sourly blaming the influence of wives and daughters for the anxiety of some families to experience the excitement of social life in the capital:

How comfortable long and happy, might gentry reside
at *their own good* houses in the country: and perhaps,
for some years, some do: till madame, getting the upper
hand, and urging the old motives of *education* for the
girls and of stirring interest for the boys, drives the
unhappy unresisting husband to crawl thro' his
shorten'd, latter, days, miserably, in a dog hole in
Marybone parish!
  A well spent country life should consist in farming,
gardening, fishing, riding, and in reading old and new
authors – what more . . . is to be wish'd for? For all the
rest is scandal, folly, madness! Even the littleness of
country sports exceed, surely, the wicked idleness of
London occupations!

> C. Bruyn Andrews and Fanny Andrews (eds), *The
> Torrington Diaries* (1954), pp.474-75.

But it was the railways which most seriously undermined
the squirearchy's traditional attachment to rural life. They
offered a cheap and easy means of conveying families from the
limited social circle of the country house and market town.
'Railroads have brought temptations in the way of many who
can neither afford to go to London nor resist it', observed
Surtees sternly. 'From Epsom over Ascot is generally the time
of their coming, whereby they have the additional opportunity
of being "done" over the races or in a gambling booth, or both.
The result . . . is that, though our Squire gets "up and down"
very cheaply, he still spends a great deal more money than he
anticipated; money that he would never have thought of
spending if it hadn't been for the confounded railway running
near his house and making the journey so easy'. (E.D. Cuming
ed., *Town and Country Papers by Robert Smith Surtees* (1929),
pp.197-98.)
  But, as we shall see, Surtees' view was too pessimistic.
Interest in foxhunting, game preservation, fishing and other
field sports persisted on a large scale to the end of the century,
despite the diversions offered by London. Equally there was a
growing recognition that by meeting together with their
fellows, the attitudes and interests of country gentlemen could

be broadened in ways which benefited their home communities on their return. William Howitt was one who took that more positive stance:

> Much has been said of the evil effect of this aristocratic habit, of spending so much time in the metropolis; of the vast sums there spent in ostentatious rivalry, in equipage and establishments; in the dissipations of theatres, operas, routes, and gaming-houses; and unquestionably, there is much truth in it. On the other hand, it cannot be denied that this annual assembling together has some advantages. A great degree of knowledge and refinement results from it, amid all the attendant folly and extravagance. The wealthy are brought into contact with vast numbers of their equals and superiors, and that sullen and haughty habit of reserve is worn off, which is always contracted by those who live in solitary seclusion, in the midst of vast estates, with none but tenants and dependents around them. They are also brought into contact with men of talent, and intelligence. They move amongst books and works of art, and are induced by different motives to become patrons and possessors of these things. If they spend large sums in splendid houses and establishments in town, such houses and such establishments become equally necessary to them in the country; and it is by this means that, instead of old and dreary castles and chateaus, we have such beautiful mansions, so filled with rich paintings and elegant furniture, dispersed all over England. From these places, as centres existing here and there, similar tastes are spread through the less wealthy classes, and the elegancies of life flow into the parsonages, cottages, and abodes of persons of less income and less intercourse with society. In town, undoubtedly, a vast number of the aristocracy spend their time and money very foolishly; but it is equally true, that many others spend theirs very beneficially to the country. Men of fortune from all quarters of the kingdom there meet, and everything which regards the improvement of their estates is discussed. . . . They

make acquaintances, and these acquaintances lead to visits, in which they observe, and copy all that can add to the embellishment of their abodes, and the value and productiveness of their gardens and estates.

William Howitt, *The Rural Life of England* (1838),
Vol. I, pp.25-27.

It was doubtless part of this same 'civilising' process that libraries, picture galleries and music rooms were becoming increasingly common features of country houses. By 1806 a library was described as 'an appendage which no man of rank or fortune can now be without, if he possesses or wishes to be thought to possess taste or genius'.

In the nineteenth century these trends were reinforced by the growing availability of newspapers and parish reading rooms for the humbler members of rural society and by the coming of railway excursions to enable them to make day trips to the seaside or a larger town. In this way rural life was enriched, while among the landed classes and clergy in particular a greater sense of personal responsibility and moral duty was gradually developed. It is to the changing attitudes towards religion and the Church that we must now turn.

Religion and the Power of Superstition

By the mid-eighteenth century religion no longer played the central role in the lives of the mass of the people that it had done a hundred years earlier. This loss of missionary zeal was particularly apparent within the established Church, with men often appointed to livings by the crown or powerful lay patrons, according to their political or social views rather than their religious fitness. Even in the nineteenth century Lady Lufton chose the Reverend Mark Robarts for the Framley benefice largely because of his close friendship with her son.

> Her tendencies were High Church, and she was enabled to perceive that those of young Mark Robarts ran in the same direction. She was very desirous that her son

should make an associate of his clergyman, and by this step she would ensure . . . that. She was anxious that the parish vicar should be one with whom she could herself fully co-operate, and was perhaps unconsciously wishful that he might in some measure be subject to her influence. Should she appoint an elder man, this might probably not be the case to the same extent; and should her son have the gift, it might probably not be the case at all. And, therefore, it was resolved that the living should be given to young Robarts.

Anthony Trollope, *Framley Parsonage* (1860), p.3.

Still more serious was the fact that well into the nineteenth century more than half the parishes of the country lacked a resident incumbent. Not until the passage of the Plurality Act of 1838 did a change become apparent. This prohibited the holding of more than two livings by a single individual and laid down a maximum of ten miles as the distance that could lie between them. It was reinforced by further legislation in 1850, which made it unlawful for any cleric to hold two benefices more than three miles apart or where the living of one of them was more than £100 per annum.

In the meantime it had been against the indifference and neglect of many eighteenth-century parsons that John Wesley, himself an Anglican cleric, had bitterly inveighed. He had begun his preaching campaign in the late 1730s, exhorting his hearers to seek salvation through faith. Hymn-singing formed an important part of Methodist worship from the beginning and deep emotions were frequently aroused. Wesley's own journals reveal the highly charged atmosphere in which prayer meetings were conducted, as on 18 July 1759, when he was preaching around Cambridge:

We called at the house where Mr. B[erridge] had been preaching in the morning, and found several there rejoicing in God and several mourning after Him. While I prayed with them many crowded into the house, some of whom burst into a strange, involuntary laughter, so that my voice could scarce be heard, and when I strove to speak louder a sudden hoarseness seized me. Then the laughter increased. I perceived it was Satan, and resolved to pray on. Immediately the Lord rebuked him that laughter was at an end, and so was my hoarseness. A vehement wrestling with God ran through the whole company . . . till, beside the three young women of the house, one young man and a girl about eleven years old, who had been counted one of the wickedest in Harlston, were exceedingly blessed with the consolations of God. . . .

We walked hence to the middle of Shelford Moor, and, seeing no person but a young woman who kept sheep, the solitude invited us to stop and sing a hymn, the sound thereof reached her. She came up slowly, weeping as she came, and then stood by a brook of water over against us with the tears running down her cheeks apace. We sang another hymn for this mourner in Sion, and wrestled for her with God in prayer.

Nehemiah Curnock (ed.), *The Journal of John Wesley* (1909), Vol. IV, pp.337-38.

For many years Wesley sought to work within the Church of England, but when this proved impossible the Wesleyans began to ordain their own ministers, from 1784. Soon local Methodist societies appeared, using lay preachers as well as ministers, and arousing the anger of many Church of England clergymen. They believed that they alone had the right to instruct the people in religious matters and feared the new movement would undermine their influence. Their dislike of dissent also extended to older Nonconformist sects like the Baptists and Congregationalists.

One who shared this hostility was George Crabbe, the Suffolk-born poet and cleric, who became rector of Muston, Leicestershire, as well as incumbent of the nearby parish of Allington, Lincolnshire, in 1789. He owed his preferment to the influence of the Dowager Duchess of Rutland, and his flattering comments about his patrons called forth the mocking contempt of William Hazlitt: 'the only leaf of his books where honour, beauty, worth, or pleasure bloom, is that inscribed to the Rutland family!' (*The Spirit of the Age* (1825), p.333.)

However, in 1794 Crabbe decided to return to his beloved Suffolk, placing a curate at Muston. Then, at the end of the century, with the bishops becoming increasingly uneasy at the growth of non-residence and plurality within the Church, all non-residents were urged to return to their livings. In these circumstances the reluctant Crabbe went back to Muston in 1805. Unfortunately, during his absence the strength of the established Church had waned and that of Methodism had waxed. This doubtless gave an added acerbity to comments upon 'Sects and Professions in Religion' in his major work, *The Borough*. It is significant that he strongly defended the pre-eminent Anglican position, and the 'robes and titles' associated with it.

> 'Sects in Religion?' – Yes, of every race
> We nurse some portion in our favour'd place;
> Not one warm preacher of one growing sect
> Can say our Borough treats him with neglect;
> Frequent as fashions they with us appear,
> And you might ask, 'how think we for the year?'
> They come to us as riders in a trade,
> And with much art exhibit and persuade.

*   *   *

> Men are not equal, and 'tis meet and right
> That robes and titles our respect excite;
> Order requires it; 'tis by vulgar pride
> That such regard is censured and denied,
> Or by that false enthusiastic zeal,
> That thinks the spirit will the priest reveal,
> And show to all men, by their powerful speech,
> Who are appointed and inspired to teach.
> Alas! could we the dangerous rule believe,
> Whom for their teacher should the crowd receive?
> Since all the varying kinds demand respect,
> All press you on to join their chosen sect,
> Although but in this single point agreed,
> 'Desert your churches and adopt our creed.'

*   *   *

A sect remains, which though divided long
In hostile parties, both are fierce and strong,
And into each enlists a warm and zealous throng.
Soon as they rose in fame, the strife arose,
The Calvinistic these, th' Arminian those;
With Wesley some remain'd, the remnant Whitfield
  chose.
Now various leaders both the parties take,
And the divided hosts their new divisions make.
  See yonder preacher to his people pass,
Borne up and swell'd by tabernacle-gas;
Much he discourses, and of various points,
All unconnected, void of limbs and joints;
He rails, persuades, explains, and moves the will,
By fierce bold words, and strong mechanic skill.

George Crabbe, *The Borough* (1810), Letter IV,
ll.1-8; 94-107; 262-75.

Gradually, however, among members of the Evangelical wing of the Church of England some of this hostility abated, and by the 1830s and 1840s there were those like the Reverend William Andrew who could praise the work the Nonconformists had carried out. In 1834 Andrew became curate of Witchingham, Norfolk, and complained bitterly of the neglect that he found: 'I have exchanged a people among whom the Gospel has sounded loudly for fourteen years, for another who scarcely know the meaning of the term; .... The Methodists perhaps have preserved the people from heathenism'. (Quoted in Owen Chadwick, *Victorian Miniature* (1960), p.29.) But despite these occasional tributes relations between Church and Dissent remained uneasy in most rural parishes to the end of the nineteenth century, with the Anglican clergy claiming the sole right of instruction and guidance of their flock, free from the interference of other sects.

Another fertile source of discontent between clerics and the Nonconformist members of their congregations arose over the question of tithes. These were traditionally levied upon the produce of the soil and were collected in both cash and kind. Where Dissent was strong, disputes were especially likely to occur. Thus at Camerton, Somerset, where John Skinner was rector from 1800 until his death in 1839, he had numerous quarrels with his parishioners over tithes as well as other matters. A particular point of contention concerning the former arose in September 1824 with a Roman Catholic farmer named Samuel Day, as Skinner noted in his journal:

> I walked up to the Glebe and saw the stadling prepared for the barley . . . I asked Cook whether he had received notice for tithing to-day. He answered in the negative, but said he supposed he should when the dew was off the grain. While we were conversing Day's wagon passed the lane in front of my premises to go into the field, and I asked whether there was any of Day's barley tithed since yesterday evening. To which he replied no . . . I then walked into 'Stanley's' field where the barley was cut and saw there was none set up in cock for tithing. I then said I should not consent to take the tithe unless the cocks were entirely separate and distinct from each other, for if my men only took it up with a pitch and no rake I must be a considerable loser. . . . I then said I knew not what Mr. Day's religion taught him, but mine instructed me to do unto others what I should expect them to do unto me, and that Mr. Day, if he were in my place, would not wish his tithe to be set out in this manner. . . .
>
> On Day's coming into the field he walked up to the wagon near which I was standing, and said to the carter, 'What is all this about? Why do you not go on hauling?' The carter replied, 'Mr. Skinner objected to the tithing of the barley.' Day then said, 'You go and tithe it, never mind what that fellow says!' The carter accordingly got some boughs and began tithing the wake. I said I never would abide by such tithing, as the cocks were not separate from each other. Day said, 'Never mind him, go on.' . . . The air of the man was in the extreme menacing; he put his face quite up to mine, shaking his head. . . . I was scarcely able to restrain myself from striking him.

Howard and Peter Coombs (eds), *John Skinner: Journal of a Somerset Rector 1803-1834*, pp.272-73.

Not until 1836 did the Tithe Commutation Act establish a set formula to eliminate some of the worst vagaries of the tithing system and end payments in kind. Even then difficulties remained. Nonconformists continued to resent having to pay to support a Church they did not attend, and tithe disputes were to tarnish Church/lay relations into the present century.

Methodism and the new spirit which it had evoked within the Church of England had, then, led to a resurgence of religious influence during the late eighteenth century and beyond, despite the various interdenominational disputes and bickering. Yet at the same time many of the old superstitions also lingered on in country parishes. John Clare in *The Village Minstrel* described the experiences of Lubin, the labourer's son and hero of the poem, in this regard:

How ancient dames a fairy's anger fear'd,
From gossips' stories Lubin often heard;
How they but every night the hearth-stone clear'd,
And 'gainst their visits all things neat prepar'd,
As fays naught more than cleanliness regard;

*   *   *

And thousands such the village keeps alive:
Beings that people superstitious earth,
That e'er in rural manners will survive,
As long as wild rusticity has birth

*   *   *

He had his dreads and fears, and scarce could pass
A churchyard's dreary mounds at silent night,
But footsteps trampled through the rustling grass,
And ghosts 'hind grave-stones peer'd in sheets of white,

*   *   *

And round his fields lay many a spot to dread;
'Twould note a history down to mark them all:
Oft monsters have been seen without a head;
And market-men oft got a dangerous fall,
When startled horses saw the sweeping pall
On the cross-roads where 'love-lorn Luce' was lain;

John Clare, *The Village Minstrel* (1821), ll.73-77;
82-85; 91-94; 370-75.

Far more disturbing, however, than this belief in spectres, goblins and other malign influences, were the cases involving witchcraft, with villagers showing an alarming readiness to blame a neighbour for the natural misfortunes of their daily life. Old people who were suspected of possessing the 'evil eye' could have their lives made a misery by these baseless allegations. Thus at Mears Ashby, Northamptonshire, in 1785 a woman was 'ducked' because she was suspected of being a witch. It was argued that if she floated, she must be guilty, but this unhappy victim, on being thrown into the pond, immediately sank and was with difficulty saved. 'On which the cry was, *No witch! No witch!* and the woman met with pity!' So reads the account in *The Gentleman's Magazine* (Vol. LV, Part 2, 1785, p.658).

In the nineteenth century such open displays of mob violence against supposed witches were frowned upon but belief in their powers nonetheless continued. A Norfolk woman, who admitted wounding a neighbour with a knife during September 1846, openly expressed her willingness 'to suffer any penalty which petty sessions might impose' because she believed she had cured herself of illness by drawing blood from someone she considered a witch. Still more frightening was an account which appeared in *The Gentleman's Magazine* in 1811. In this case a 77-year-old suspect, Betty Townsend, was charged at Taunton Assizes with obtaining money from a child:

> The prosecutor, Jacob Poole, a poor labouring man, . . . had been in the habit of sending his daughter, aged about 13, with apples in a basket to market. About Jan. 24 last, the old woman met with the little girl, and

asked to see what she had in her basket, which having examined, she said to her, 'Hast got any money?' The child said she had none. 'Then get some for me,' said the old woman, 'and bring it to me at the Castle door (a tavern in Taunton), or I will kill thee!' The child, terrified to an extreme at such a threat from a witch, procured 2s. and carried it to her, when the old woman said, ''Tis a good turn thou hast got it, or else I would have made thee die by inches.' This was repeated seven times within five months, when Poole (the father) going to the shop of Mr. Bruford, a druggist in Taunton, to pay a little bill which he owed for medicine, found . . . that different small sums . . . had been borrowed by the girl in her father's name, for the purpose, as she said, of going to market, but carried as a peace-offering to the old woman. The whole was now discovered; and Poole's wife and another woman took the girl with them to the prisoner's house, and interrogated her as to the facts. She admitted a knowledge of the girl, but . . . swore that if they dared accuse her, she would make them 'die by inches.' – 'No,' said Mrs. Poole, . . . 'that thee shall not; I'll hinder that;' and, taking a pin from her clothes, scratched the witch from her elbow to her wrist, in three places, to *draw her blood*, a process believed to be of unfailing efficacy as an antidote to witchcraft. The idea of this wicked woman's power has had such an effect on the mind of the girl, that she is now . . . scarcely able to take any sustenance. The Jury found the prisoner guilty; and the Judge observed, that only her extreme old age prevented him from pronouncing on her the severest sentence the law would allow; she was sentenced to pay a fine of 1s. and to be kept to hard labour in the House of Correction for six calendar months.

The Gentleman's Magazine, Vol. LXXXI, Part 2, 1811, pp.183-84.

Belief in magic and in the influence of omens was one way of emphasising people's helplessness in the face of an unpredictable and possibly malevolent fate. At a time when medical treatment was rudimentary and death rates high, it seemed only prudent to many that they should take all possible steps to placate evil spirits and to ostracise, or even ill-treat, those suspected of exercising harmful powers. Only the spread of education and an end to what John Clare called 'wild rusticity' could eradicate such practices. Religious influences alone were insufficient.

Schools and Schooling

Apart from its possible effect in countering undesirable superstitious beliefs, however, elementary education was seen by many in authority as a way of producing a disciplined, honest and hard-working labour force. Far less attention was paid to its role in developing fresh ideas or imparting knowledge. Indeed, there were those, like Colonel John Byng, who were firmly opposed to all academic instruction for the lower orders: 'I have met some of the newly-adopted Sunday-schools today', he wrote in June 1790, 'and seen others in their schools; I am point blank against these institutions; the poor shou'd not read, and of writing I never heard, for them, the use'. Earlier he had suggested that it was from books that the poor learned immorality, while 'forgery was . . . the consequence of learning to write'. (C. Bruyn Andrews and Fanny Andrews eds, *The Torrington Diaries* (1954), pp.198, 246.) Much the same approach was adopted by the fictional Dr Folliott, when he blamed the 1830 'Swing' riots and the upsurge in crime upon too much schooling: 'The policeman, who was sent down to examine, says my house has been broken open on the most scientific principles. All this comes of education . . . . Robbery perhaps comes of poverty, but scientific principles of robbery come of education. I suppose the learned friend has written a sixpenny treatise on mechanics, and the rascals who robbed me have been reading it.' (Thomas Love Peacock, *Crotchet Castle* (1831), pp.242-43.)

Even those who favoured a wider educational provision were firm on the limits within which it should operate. Thus the first annual report of the National Society for Promoting the Education of the Poor in the Principles of the Established

Church declared in 1812 that its sole object was 'to communicate to the poor generally . . . such knowledge and habits, as are sufficient to guide them through life, in their proper stations, . . . and to train them to the performance of their religious duties by early discipline'. Even in 1857 when schooling had become widely available, Bishop Wilberforce told a meeting of the Oxford Diocesan Association of Schoolmasters that 'there was, perhaps, too much outcry against children being taken from School early to work on farms', adding frankly that they 'did not want everybody to be learned men, or to make everybody unfit for following the plough, or else the rest of us would have nothing to eat.'

In the early days many village children who received an education attended private or 'dame' schools of the kind described by George Crabbe:

> To every class we have a school assign'd,
> Rules for all ranks and food for every mind;
> Yet one there is, that small regard to rule
> Or study pays, and still is deem'd a school:
> That, where a deaf, poor, patient widow sits,
> And awes some thirty infants as she knits;
> Infants of humble, busy wives, who pay
> Some trifling price for freedom through the day.
>
> *   *   *
>
> Her room is small, they cannot widely stray –
> Her threshold high, they cannot run away;
> Though deaf, she sees the rebel-heroes shout; –
> Though lame, her white rod nimbly walks about;
> With band of yarn she keeps offenders in,
> And to her gown the sturdiest rogue can pin.
> Aided by these, and spells, and tell-tale birds,
> Her power they dread and reverence her words.

George Crabbe, *The Borough* (1810), Letter XXIV,
ll.1-8; 11-18.

Rather more ambitious were the establishments financed at least partly by charity, as many National Schools were. In these strong religious and moral overtones were to be found, such as applied in schools instituted by Hannah More and her sisters at Blagden in Somerset. Hannah, a devout Anglican, was a prolific writer of tracts and pamphlets, and in 1801 in a letter to the Bishop of Bath and Wells she summarised her instructional philosophy:

> When I settled in this country thirteen years ago, I found the poor in many of the villages sunk in a deplorable state of ignorance and vice. There were, I think, no Sunday schools in the whole district, except one in my own parish, which had been established by our respectable rector, and another in the adjoining parish of Churchill. This drew me to the more neglected villages ... . Not one school here did I ever attempt to establish without the hearty concurrence of the clergyman of the parish. My plan of instruction is extremely simple and limited. They learn, on week-days, such coarse works as may fit them for servants. I allow of no writing for the poor. My object is not to make fanatics, but to train up the lower classes in habits of industry and piety. I knew no way of teaching morals but by teaching principles; and of inculcating Christian principles without a good knowledge of scripture. ... Finding that what the children learned at school they commonly lost at home by the profaneness and ignorance of their parents, it occurred to me in some of the larger parishes to invite the latter to come at six on the Sunday evening, for an hour, to the school, together with the elder scholars. A plain printed sermon and a printed prayer is read to them, and a psalm is sung. ...
>
> For many years I have given away annually, nearly two hundred Bibles, Common Prayer Books, and Testaments. To teach the poor to read without providing them with *safe* books, has always appeared to me an improper measure, and this consideration induced me to enter upon the laborious undertaking of the Cheap Repository Tracts. ...
>
> William Roberts, *Memoirs of the Life and Correspondence of Mrs. Hannah More* (1834), Vol. 3, pp.133-35.

In such restricted circumstances village school teachers were held in low esteem, with the post often undertaken by those too sick, too old or too incompetent to earn their living in any other way. Mary Russell Mitford was not alone when in 1819 she described the position of country schoolmaster as a 'wretched and helpless trade'. Significantly in *Jane Eyre*, when St John Rivers suggested that Jane should take up a post as schoolmistress in the village where he was incumbent, he felt the need to apologise for making the offer:

> 'I believe you will accept the post I offer you,' said he; 'and hold it for a while: not permanently, though: any more than I could permanently keep the narrow and narrowing – the tranquil, hidden office of English country incumbent . . . .'
>
> 'Do explain,' I urged, when he halted once more.
>
> 'I will; and you shall hear how poor the proposal is – how trivial – how cramping. I shall not stay long at Morton . . . but while I *do* stay, I will exert myself to the utmost for its improvement. Morton, when I came to it two years ago, had no school: the children of the poor were excluded from every hope of progress. I established one for boys: I mean now to open a second school for girls. I have hired a building for the purpose, with a cottage of two rooms attached to it for the mistress's house. Her salary will be thirty pounds a year: her house is already furnished, very simply, but sufficiently, by the kindness of a lady, Miss Oliver; the only daughter of the sole rich man in my parish . . . . The same lady pays for the education and clothing of an orphan from the workhouse; on condition that she shall aid the mistress in such menial offices connected with her own house and the school, as her occupation of teaching will prevent her having time to discharge in person. Will you be this mistress?'
>
> He put the question rather hurriedly; he seemed half to expect an indignant, or at least a disdainful rejection of the offer: . . . . In truth it was humble – but then it was sheltered, and I wanted a safe asylum: it was plodding – but then, compared with that of a governess

in a rich house, it was independent; . . . it was not ignoble – not unworthy – not mentally degrading. I made my decision.

'I thank you for the proposal, Mr. Rivers; and I accept it with all my heart.'

'But you comprehend me?' he said. 'It is a village-school: your scholars will be only poor girls – cottagers' children – at the best, farmers' daughters. Knitting, sewing, reading, writing, cyphering, will be all you will have to teach. What, will you do with your accomplishments? What with the largest portion of your mind – sentiments – tastes?'

'Save them till they are wanted. They will keep.' . . .

It is evening. I have dismissed, with the fee of an orange, the little orphan who serves me as a handmaid. I am sitting alone on the hearth. This morning, the village school opened. I had twenty scholars. But three of the number can read: none write or cypher. Several knit, and a few sew a little. They speak with the broadest accent of the district. At present, they and I have a difficulty in understanding each other's language. Some of them are unmannered, rough, intractable, as well as ignorant; but others are docile, have a wish to learn, and evince a disposition that pleases me. I must not forget that these coarsely-clad little peasants are of flesh and blood as good as the scions of gentlest genealogy; and that the germs of native excellence, refinement, intelligence, kind feeling, are as likely to exist in their hearts as in those of the best-born. My duty will be to develope these germs: . . . .

Charlotte Brontë, *Jane Eyre* (1847), pp.359-60; 363.

As the daughter of a country clergyman Charlotte Brontë was well able to appreciate the intellectual limitations of village life and to make due allowance for them.

Not until 1833 did the state provide its first grant of £20 000 to elementary education, while the appointment of the first of HM Inspectors of Schools followed six years later. But even then the process of raising the standard of instruction in village schools proved pitifully slow. In 1841-42 Mr S. Tremenheere, one of the first two HMIs to be appointed, reported gloomily on the 'many defects' he had found in schools in Norfolk:

> Particular Illustrations might be taken from almost every School which I inspected or visited with those interested in it. In one, Twenty Boys who had been Two Years at the School could not read Words of Four Letters correctly; . . . . In a Second, Thirty Boys who had been from Eighteen Months to Two Years at the School, and were nearly old enough to be taken away to work, could not read a Verse in the New Testament without Hesitation and Mistakes. In a Third, Fifteen Boys from Ten to Twelve Years of Age, in the First Class, read with a Boldness and Fluency which seemed to impose on the Master, who allowed them to pass over connecting Words, Signs of Tenses, and smaller Obstacles, in their Progress to the longer Words, which he always repeated after them, sometimes before. When examined in Scripture History, only One Boy could answer any One Question, and his Knowledge did not enable him to say who led the Children of Israel into the Promised Land. . . . They did not know what County joined their own, nor the Direction of London, nor in what Quarter the Sun was in the Middle of the Day, nor the Direction of East, West, North, and South. These were Boys just about to leave School, and who will be said to have 'received their Education' at a School supported at some Expense by a large resident Landowner.

> *Minutes of the Committee of Council on Education,*
> Parl. Papers 1842, Vol. 33, p.209.

Apart from such obvious deficiencies, a further handicap to the spread of efficient rural schools was the fact that often the children were kept away as soon as they were offered employment. Many of the tasks they undertook were lonely and uninteresting, providing little stimulus to their mind and thereby encouraging the slowness of speech and intellect which critics claimed were characteristic of young villagers. Only in the north of England, where adult wage rates were higher and family circumstances more secure, was a greater value placed on education. In pastoral districts, too, where there was a limited demand for child labour, the problems were also less acute. But in most counties children of seven or eight would be engaged in casual field work during much of the spring, summer and early autumn, and at the age of about ten would normally leave school for good. 'Bird-keeping is the earliest work at which boys are employed', wrote the rector of Bryanston-cum-Durweston, Dorset, in 1842. 'Their next stage in labour is the watching cattle or poultry in the field; for this purpose more personal activity is required. Their next step in life is driving the plough, and assisting the carter in the stable, &c.; and then comes the actual holding [of the] plough, mowing, ditching, and the usual work of a regular farm-labourer.' Significantly, he also added: 'For my own part, as soon as a boy is capable of taking any situation, which whilst it may afford him some wages at the same time initiates him into the calling by which he is in the end to gain his bread, and gradually inures him to that exposure to the weather which must form a part of his lot, I am glad to see him obtain one.' (*Report of Special Assistant Poor Law Commissioners on the Employment of Women and Children in Agriculture*, Parl. Papers 1843, Vol. 12, pp.72-74.)

Elsewhere children remained at home because they lacked suitable clothing or footwear or because their parents were unable to afford the weekly fee of 1d. or 2d. which attendance demanded. This applied especially after the 1834 Poor Law Amendment Act ended both child allowances from the poor rates and occasional payment of the school fees of the neediest children. In areas where cottage industries, like lacemaking or straw plaiting, flourished these too adversely affected school attendance and literacy levels. In 1840 Bedfordshire and Hertfordshire, two noted centres for straw plait, had the lowest male literacy rates in the whole country.

Nevertheless, by the 1850s elementary education had been accepted as having a major role to play in providing moral guidance and social discipline for the labouring classes. In this respect it was seen as an important adjunct of organised religion.

Communal Activities and Entertainments

An increasingly popular method of encouraging a spirit of self-dependence among the lower orders, alongside religion and education, was the promotion of friendly societies. Not only did county agricultural societies often give prizes to men and women who had long been members of these clubs, but landowners, clergy and farmers regularly subscribed to them, to boost their funds. Weekly contributions to such organisations by labourers and artisans were felt to encourage prudent attitudes, as well as offering much-needed financial aid at times of sickness or death, through the benefits they provided. As the rector of Pewsey, Wiltshire, wrote in 1786, 'The system of Friendly Societies should be pushed as far as it will go'.

Significantly, through their rule books most of the societies also exercised a firm control over members' conduct. One club at Shepton Beauchamp, Somerset, for example, declared piously in 1802: 'We hereby Promise to behave Ourselves on all Occasions religiously, honestly and soberly, to promote and encourage Virtue and Godly living, and to suppress and detect Vice, immorality, profaneness, Drunkenness, and debauchery, to the utmost of our power and likewise to attend our places of worship on the sabbath days'. At Meare in the same county members were threatened with the formidable fine of 2s. 6d. if they were 'guilty of drunkenness, cursing, swearing or using uncivil language or if they spoke words reflecting on the Government, argued about religion or state affairs, quarrelled, gambled or challenged another member about trade or business'. (Margaret Fuller, *West Country Friendly Societies* (1964), p.62.)

Although many friendly societies were already established at the beginning of the nineteenth century, their membership was boosted by the passage of the 1834 Poor Law Amendment Act. Faced with the deterrent approach of that legislation, artisans and labourers resolved ever more firmly to render one another financial help in times of sickness, accident or death rather than apply to the Poor Law union for help. But alongside these benefit functions the clubs had an important social role. At their meetings, often held in a public house, members could discuss matters of common interest, while a society's annual feast day was frequently the most important event in a village's year. Members, dressed in their best clothes and wearing ribbons and rosettes in the club colours, would march to church, preceded by banners and a band. There they attended a service, before walking in procession to the club meeting place, where a dinner awaited them. Often the celebration would take place on Whit Monday:

> All work has ceased. There has been, at first, a sabbath stillness, a repose, a display of holiday costume. Groups of men have met here and there in the streets in quiet talk; the children have begun to play, and make their shrill voices heard through the hamlets. There have been stalls of sweetmeats and toys set out in the little market-place, on the green, by the shady walk, or under the well-known tree. Suddenly the bells have struck up a joyous peal . . . . Forth comes streaming the village procession of hardy men or comely women, all arrayed in their best, gay with ribbons and scarfs, a band of music sounding before them; their broad banner of peace and union flapping over their heads, and their wands shouldered like the spears of an ancient army, or used as walking-staves. Forth they stream from their club-room at the village ale-house . . . making the procession of the town before they go to church, and then again after church and before going to dinner . . . . In front of them comes bearing the great banner, emblazoned with some fitting scene and motto, old Harry Lomax the blacksmith, deputed to that office for the brawny strength of his arms, and yet, if the wind be stirring, evidently staggering under its weight, and finding enough to do to hold it aloft. There it floats its length of blue and yellow, and on its top nods the huge posy of peonies, laburnum flowers, and lilacs . . . . Then comes sounding the band of drums, bassoons, hautboys, flutes, and clarionets: then the honorary members – the freeholders of the place – the sage apothecary, and the priest . . . – and then the simple sons of the hamlet, walking as stately and as gravely as

they can for the nods and smiles of all their neighbours who do not join in the procession, but are all at door and window to see them go by. There they go, passing down the shady lane with all the village children at their heels, to the next hamlet, half a mile off, which furnishes members to the club, and must therefore witness their glory . . .; their music comes merrily up the hill; and as it dies away at the next turn, the drumming of distant villages becomes audible in half a dozen different quarters.

William Howitt, *The Rural Life of England* (1838),
Vol. 2, pp.183-88.

Once the meal had ended, toasts were drunk and then a dance would frequently round off the proceedings:

> An' when tha took awoy the dishes,
> Tha drink'd good healths, an' wish'd good wishes,
> To all the girt vo'kes o' the land,
> An' all good things vo'ke took in hand;

*   *   *

> An' a'ter that they went all out
> In rank agien, an' wa'k'd about,
> An' gi'ed zome parish vo'ke a call;
> An' then went down to Narley Hall
> An' had zome beer, an' danc'd between
> The elem trees upon the green.
> An' gwain along the road, tha done
> All sarts o' mad-cap things var fun;
> An' danc'd, a-poken out ther poles,
> An' pushen buoys down into holes:
> An' Sammy Stubbs come out o' rank,
> An' kiss'd I up agien the bank,
> A sassy chap; I ha'nt vargi'ed en
> Not eet, – in shart, I han't a-zeed en.

William Barnes, *Poems of Rural Life in the Dorset
Dialect* (1847), 'Whitsuntide an' Club Walken',
ll.45-48; 55-67.

Friendly society celebrations were by tradition associated with Whitsuntide but there were other festivities with seasonal connections, like May Day, when the children paraded the village with their garlands, or Christmas with its carol singers and mummers. Wordsworth recalled the warm sense of community which such events could engender:

> The Minstrels played their Christmas tune
> To-night beneath my cottage-eaves;
> While, smitten by a lofty moon,
> The encircling laurels, thick with leaves,
> Gave back a rich and dazzling sheen,
> That overpowered their natural green

>   *   *   *

> And who but listened? – till was paid
> Respect to every Inmate's claim:
> The greeting given, the music played,
> In honour of each household name,
> Duly pronounced with lusty call,
> And 'Merry Christmas' wished to all!

>   *   *   *

> For pleasure hath not ceased to wait
> On these expected annual rounds;
> Whether the rich man's sumptuous gate
> Call forth the unelaborate sounds,
> Or they are offered at the door
> That guards the lowliest of the poor.

> William Wordsworth, 'To the Rev. Dr.
> Wordsworth' (1819), ll.1-6; 13-18; 31-36.

Contrasted with these were less respectable recreations, like bull- and badger-baiting and cock-fighting. This latter attracted all classes, and well into the first quarter of the nineteenth century notices appeared in provincial newspapers advertising 'gentlemen's cock-fights'. Not until the beginning

of Victoria's reign did a general revulsion against these
barbarous sports lead to their virtual disappearance from
respectable circles. Cock-fighting was finally made illegal in
1849, although it certainly continued clandestinely after that
date. But in earlier years, it – and other rough games and
amusements – had sometimes featured at village feasts.
Compared to such entertainments as these, village cricket
matches, quoits or even football contests seemed tame and
respectable.

Some of the celebrations had their sexual implications as
well. Many a match, it was said, was made at a hiring fair, when
farm servants and maids stood around seeking fresh
employment. For once that business had been concluded, they
were free to enjoy the entertainment offered, as a north-
country ballad described:

> Oh, lads and lasses hither come
> To Wrekington to see the fun,
> An' mind ye bring yor Sunday shun,
>   There'll be rare wark wi' dancin-O.
>
> The fiddler's elbow wagg'd a' neet,
> He thought he wad drop of his seet,
> For deel a bit they'd let him eat,
>   They were se keen of dancin-O;
>
> Now they danc't agyen till it was day,
> An' then went hyem, but by the way,
> There was some had rare fun they say,
>   An' found it nine months after-O;

> 'Wrekington Hiring' ll.1-4; 25-28; 41-44 in
> *Collection of Broadsides, etc.* at the British Library,
> 1875. d.13.

But if fairs and village feasts provided the pinnacle of most
rural parishes' social life, for agriculturalists it was the harvest
which formed the summit of their yearly work-cycle, at least in
arable districts. Inevitably it attracted to itself celebrations,
which began even before the operation itself had commenced.

Typical of the procedure adopted was that at Debenham, Suffolk, in the first half of the nineteenth century:

> The harvest was generally agreed for the gathering in . . . some weeks before it began, either to board the men during the time or pay all in money and the bargain concluded with a pint or quart of strong ale to each man.
>
> One was selected from amongst themselves as 'My Lord', the oldest workman on the farm if able, and one also for 'My Lady' who went next him. My Lord took the lead in the field and a forfeiture was the consequence of any attempt to get before him. All were bound also to keep within a short distance of him, that is to say about a 'couple of clips', equal to about half a sheaf. Friends and strangers who went into the field were asked for a largess & for this if wished they would express their thanks by what they called 'hallowing it'. [i.e. hallooing] . . .
>
> The harvest ended, then came the Horkey. . . . The supper began at six and the drinking & smoking finished at 12, to which only the men came. In some places their wives & families were also invited. Extra helps also sometimes joined them, such as the wheelwright, carpenter, blacksmith, collarmaker & tailor & partook of the same fare. . . . My Lord usually took the head of the table and my Lady sat next him on his right, the rest sitting as they followed each other in the field. The feast consisted of a profusion of cold plum pudding, pork, beef, etc. The president did not usually help all, but they helped themselves as the dishes might be placed near them. Each brought his own knife and fork, or, lacking the latter, one was soon formed of wood, a skewer which answered the purpose. I remember the large milk pail with bright iron hoops being placed upon the table filled with the best foaming harvest ale and of which they had as much to drink as they pleased. Gin & water . . ., a bowl of punch and syllabub made by milking into beer with spice and sugar was allowed late in the evening and all had pipes

and tobacco who wished for it. My Lord had the pail placed before him and he took from thence a gotch or jug full as he required it. It was poured from thence into two horns, which number sufficed, passing round to all.

Then commenced the singing. The first song generally was:

> Now supper is ended and all things are past
> Here's a Mistress good health boys in a full flowing glass.
> She is a good mistress, she provides us good cheer,
> Come all my brave boys now & drink off yar beer.

This was repeated as the horn passed to each .... Much jocularity and merriment was indulged in on the occasion. The principal topics discussed were those of their late occupation and incidents connected with it. ... In the course of the evening my Lord was called upon to dance a hornpipe to which he ... readily assented for the amusement of the company, himself humming the tune of the College Hornpipe ....

> Quoted in Joan Thirsk and Jean Imray (eds),
> *Suffolk Farming in the Nineteenth Century* (1958),
> pp.54-56.

Field Sports and Poaching

So far, in examining the leisure interests of country people, attention has been focused on activities likely to appeal to the lower orders of that society. For the landed classes, by contrast, it was hunting, shooting and fishing which formed the major recreations. As one early Victorian enthusiast declared, field sports were essential if a gentleman were to remain in the country: 'The game, the kennel, and stable, the decoy and the river, afford to the rich man recreation for every leisure hour.' (Quoted in Pamela Horn, *The Rural World* (1980), p.172.) Thus Squire Osbaldeston not only took on the mastership of a number of famous hunts during the course of a long career, but he was an expert shot and one of the best cricketers in the country. So lavish indeed was his expenditure that in 1848 his estates in Yorkshire had to be sold to pay off his debts. In old age he admitted ruefully that on a 'fair calculation' he had lost 'nearly £200,000 by betting and keeping racehorses during a period of 45 years'. (E.D. Cuming ed., *Squire Osbaldeston: His Autobiography*, 1926, p.3.)

Osbaldeston was unusually profligate, but even more modest sportsmen, like Mr Thorne of Ullathorne, devoted much time and money to their sporting concerns:

> he had supported the hunt by every means in his power. He had preserved game till no goose or turkey could show a tail in the parish of St. Ewold's. He had planted gorse covers with more care than oaks and larches. He had been more anxious for the comfort of his foxes than of his ewes and lambs. No meet had been more popular than Ullathorne; no man's stables had been more liberally open to the horses of distant men than Mr. Thorne's; no man had said more, written more, or done more to keep the club up.
>
> Anthony Trollope, *Barchester Towers* (1857), p.195.

Farmers, too, despite the possible damage caused to their crops by hunts, were often keen followers of hounds. 'In some countries, notably Lord Yarborough's', wrote E.W. Bovill, 'sixty or seventy farmers could be seen riding to hounds, all in red coats.' And in the view of Surtees those men who hunted were among the most prosperous of their class. They were major employers of labour, who arranged the day's farming programme before they saddled up and regarded hunting not just as a relaxation, but 'as a means of hearing local news' and meeting their neighbours. (Frederick Watson, *Robert Smith Surtees* (1933), p.108.)

However, the single-hearted commitment to which hunting sometimes gave rise was commented upon by a disapproving German visitor in 1828:

> Here ... people are so little shamed of the most "crasse" self-love, that an Englishman of rank once instructed me that a good "fox-hunter" must let

nothing stop him, or distract his attention when following the fox; and if his own father should be thrown in leaping a ditch, and lie there, should, he said, "if he couldn't help it," leap his horse over him, and trouble himself no more about him till the end of the chase.

E.M. Butler (ed.), *A Regency Visitor: The English Tour of Prince Pückler-Maskau, 1826-1828* (1957), p.337.

Something of the exhilaration experienced by these enthusiastic sportsmen is well conveyed by R.S. Surtees in his account of the doings of Jorrocks:

Now they are on him again, and Mr. Jorrocks thrusts his hat upon his brow, runs the fox's tooth of his hat-string through the button-hole of his roomy coat, gathers up his reins, and bustles away outside the cover, in a state of the utmost excitement – half frantic, in fact! There is a tremendous scent, and Reynard is puzzled whether to fly or stay. He tries the opposite side, but Pigg, who is planted on a hill, heads him, and he is beat off his line.

The hounds gain upon him, and there is nothing left but a bold venture up the middle, so, taking the bed of the brook, he endeavours to baffle his followers by the water. Now they splash after him, the echoing banks and yew-studded cliffs resounding to their cry. The dell narrows towards the west, and Mr. Jorrocks rides forward to view him away. A countryman yoking his plough is before him, and with hat high in air, "TALLI-HO'S" till he's hoarse. Pigg's horn on one side, and Jorrocks's on the other, get the hounds out in a crack; the countryman mounts one of his carters, the other runs away with the plough, and the three sportsmen are as near mad as anything can possibly be. It's ding, dong, hey away, pop with them all!

The fallows carry a little, but there's a rare scent, and for two miles of ill-enclosed land Reynard is scarcely a field before the hounds. Now Pigg views him! Now Jorrocks! Now Charley! Now Pigg again! Thirty couple of hounds lengthen as they go, but there is no Pomponius Ego to tell. The fox falls back at a wall, and the hounds are in the same field. He tries again – now he's over! The hounds follow, and dash forward, but the fox has turned short up the inside of the wall, and gains a momentary respite. Now they are on him again! They view him through the gateway beyond: he rolls as he goes! Another moment, and they pull him down in the middle of a large grass field!

"*Hooray! Hooray! Hooray!*" exclaims Mr. Jorrocks, rolling off his horse, and diving into the middle of the pack, and snatching the fox, which old Thunderer resents by seizing him behind, and tearing his white cords half-way down his legs. "*Hooray!*" repeats he, kicking out behind, and holding the fox over his head, his linen flying out, and his enthusiastic old face all beaming with joy. . . .

They re-enter Handley Cross by half-past nine, and at ten sit down to breakfast . . . .

R.S. Surtees, *Handley Cross* (1854), pp.498–500.

Elsewhere, however, it was game preservation which formed the principal leisure interest of landowners. The popularity of shooting – and the size of bags – increased dramatically in the early nineteenth century, thanks to the introduction of hand-rearing. On many estates a separate game department was formed, with a consequently heavy outlay in cash, and game books carefully recorded the number of deaths for posterity. At Longleat expenditure on pheasants rose from £264 in 1790 to about £400 in 1810 and £2555 by 1856, while the number of keepers also increased. During the shooting season armies of watchers were recruited from among the local labourers to keep a look-out for poachers, and there was an increasing use of dog-spears, spring-guns and man-traps to protect the preserves. Sometimes these barbarous weapons interfered with the activities of the foxhunters. The Belvoir Hunt suffered greatly from Lord Harborough's decision to close Stapleford Park to them and his enforcement of this prohibition by the deployment of dog-spears.

Among expert shots the size of bags became a matter of personal prestige. This was especially true from the early nineteenth century, when Joseph Manton, the most famous English gunmaker, perfected the flint-lock. This gave an efficient gun which was light and easy to handle. A three-day shooting party of eight guns at Ashridge, Hertfordshire, during 1823 accounted for 1088 head of game, while the peak of game licences issued was reached in 1827 when it stood at 51 375. Thereafter, there was a temporary decline in the sport's popularity, associated with poor seasons, game law agitation, and a sharp increase in the level of duty imposed. But from 1853 the upward movement was resumed.

The enjoyment experienced by two sportsmen engaged, with their two pointers, upon a shooting expedition at Creswell Crags on the Duke of Portland's estate in the late 1760s was undoubtedly shared by the far larger parties who followed their example a century later:

> Bright Sol's all chearing Beams illumines the Day,
> The Dew's exhal'd from off the spangled spray:
> Now Covies to the silent stubbles fly,
> And fearful Hares 'midst Brake and Thistle lie;
>
> See Pan and Flora range the late shorn Plain;
> Where Game abounds they seldom hunt in vain;
> By Instinct strongly urg'd each try around,
> Now Snuff the Air, now scent the tainted ground.
>
> A gentle Gale that blows along the Land
> The game betrays; the Dogs they Draw, they Stand
> Search all the Objects that afford delight,
> There's none like this can please the Fowler's sight.
>
> Softly they step expecting instant Sport,
> The Covey springs to find some safe resort
> Like Lightning flys the Shot, one falls to th' Ground,
> The rest well mark'd, again are to be found.

Sated with Sport as one recumbent lies
Success the other strews before his Eyes;
Behold what Dainties in profusion spread,
The mingled produce of the recent dead: . . . .

Verses on the frames of a series of four paintings
depicting two gentlemen on a shooting expedition
produced by George Stubbs in 1767–1770 and
exhibited at the Tate Gallery in 1984.

With the increased concern for game preservation which became apparent from the late eighteenth century there was a natural desire on the part of owners to protect their investments. It was in these circumstances that bitter clashes occurred between preservers and poachers. For in a landowner-dominated parliament it was all too easy for amendments to the Game Laws to be introduced to keep pace with the new enthusiasm for preservation. Between 1760 and 1816 thirty-three Acts reached the statute book directed against the ordinary poaching of small game. And to add to the tension, until 1831 the right to shoot game was a privilege annexed to a particular social position. All save owners of land worth £100 a year, lessees of land worth £150 a year, the eldest sons of esquires or of persons of higher degree and the owners of franchises were prohibited. But the restrictions had many anomalies. Thus the eldest son of an esquire who lacked the necessary property qualification was not debarred from shooting, although his father was. Gamekeepers too were allowed to shoot and this led to qualified men 'engaging' their unqualified relatives and friends as ostensible keepers.

Landowners, meanwhile, sought to eradicate poaching by repressive legislation. Poachers, finding themselves opposed by the law and by a growing army of gamekeepers, responded by operating increasingly at night, despite the severe penalties they faced. Eventually under the infamous Ellenborough Act of 1803 anyone who offered armed resistance to lawful arrest – and that included arrest by a keeper – could be hanged as a felon. For a time the new measure seemed to be effective. But in the misery of the post-war agricultural depression men were ready to risk the gallows rather than see their families starve. Gangs roamed the countryside and in 1817, in an attempt to tighten the screw still further, even unarmed poaching by night was made punishable by transportation for seven years. Anyone who returned within that time was to be transported for life. In the poacher's eyes transportation with its separation from home and family was only a little less terrible than the gallows and so men gathered together with still greater determination to avoid arrest. It was against this desperate background that Crabbe wrote 'Smugglers and Poachers' in 1817-18:

> Thus they proceeded, till a winter came,
> When the stern keeper told of stolen game.
> Throughout the woods the poaching dogs had been;
> And from him nothing should the robbers screen,
> From him and law – he would all hazards run,
> Nor spare a poacher, were his brother one –

> ❋   ❋   ❋

> Now was the game destroy'd, and not an hare
> Escaped at least the danger of the snare;
> Woods of their feather'd beauty were bereft,
> The beauteous victims of the silent theft;
> The well-known shops received a large supply,
> That they who could not kill at least might buy.
> James was enraged, enraged his lord, and both
> Confirm'd their threatening with a vengeful oath;
> Fresh aid was sought – and nightly on the lands
> Walk'd on their watch the strong determined bands:
> Pardon was offer'd, and a promised pay
> To him who would the desperate gang betray.
> Nor fail'd the measure – on a certain night
> A few were seized – the rest escaped by flight;
> Yet they resisted boldly ere they fled,
> And blows were dealt around, and blood was shed;
> Two groaning helpers on the earth were laid,
> When more arrived the lawful cause to aid;

Then four determined men were seized and bound,
And Robert in this desperate number found.
In prison fetter'd, he deplored his fate,
And cursed the folly he perceived too late.

George Crabbe *Tales of the Hall* (1819),
Book XXI, ll.233-38, 261-82.

Not until the late 1820s was there some easing of the situation, with a prohibition on the use of mantraps and spring-guns coming in 1827 and a new Night Poaching Act passed in 1828. Under this anyone found poaching after dark would face a maximum sentence of three months' imprisonment with hard labour, instead of the old penalty of transportation. At the end of that term he had to find a surety for himself of £10, plus two sureties of £5 each. If he could not obtain these, he had to serve a further six months in gaol. For a second offence the penalty was doubled and for a third the offender could be transported for seven years as before. An armed offender who put up resistance to arrest, however, could still be transported for seven years, even if this were his first offence, and if he had not actually captured any game, but had merely been searching for it. Three years later the archaic qualifications for shooting game were also abolished.

Yet, despite these ameliorations, conflicts between poachers and keepers persisted. As late as the 1840s the moralistic Harriet Martineau gave a salutary warning to would-be poachers of the penalties which awaited them if they persisted with their nefarious activities (*Forest and Game-Law Tales*, 1846). But poverty and hunger were powerful incentives for labouring men to take advantage of what they regarded as the largesse of the countryside. In 1844 alone there were at least nineteen serious clashes involving poaching gangs, with thirty-one people gravely wounded and two keepers murdered. Game convictions of a less serious kind also continued at a high level, rising from 2424 in 1839 to 4270 in 1844. In some counties, including Berkshire, Hertfordshire, Oxfordshire, Wiltshire, Buckinghamshire, Bedfordshire and Rutland, these offences comprised a quarter or more of *all* male summary convictions in 1843. Cases were quoted where excessive zeal on the part of magistrates had led to the imposition of illegal sentences, that is, more severe than the maximum laid down in the Game Acts. 'There is not a worse-constituted tribunal on the face of the earth', declared the Whig politician, Brougham, in 1828, '. . . than that at which summary convictions on the Game Laws constantly take place; I mean a bench or a brace of sporting justices'. They included men like Sir Simon Steeltrap, MP, JP,

> a great preserver of game and public morals. By administering the laws which he assists in making, he disposes, at his pleasure, of the land and its live stock, including all the two-legged varieties, with and without feathers, in a circumference of several miles round Steeltrap Lodge. He has enclosed commons and woodlands; . . . committed many poachers, shot a few; convicted one third of the peasantry; suspected the rest; and passed nearly the whole of them through a wholesome course of prison discipline, which has finished their education at the expense of the county.
>
> Thomas Love Peacock, *Crotchet Castle* (1831), p.167.

Small wonder that F.M.L. Thompson has noted:

> game preservation continued to make few friends outside landowners' circles, and undoubtedly made many enemies. As a sport shooting emphasized the solidarity of aristocracy and gentry, sitting together as magistrates trying poaching offences, and standing together at the butts. It also stirred the resentment of farmers and labourers and was a notable hindrance to rural harmony . . . .
>
> F.M.L. Thompson, *English Landed Society in the Nineteenth Century* (1963), p.144.

Farmers, in particular, felt aggrieved at the damage caused to their crops – and their incomes – by both ground and winged game. Reductions in rent and the payment of compensation by some landlords rarely covered the losses incurred, and not all landowners made such concessions anyway.

But perhaps the last word on poaching should be left to the agricultural trade union leader, Joseph Arch, who put forward a view shared by many of his fellow villagers during these years:

> The plain truth is, we labourers do not believe hares and rabbits belong to any individual, not any more than thrushes and blackbirds do. I should not inform against a man who knocked over a rabbit or a hare. Has the hare or the rabbit a brand on him for purposes of identification? . . .
>
> To see hares and rabbits running across his path is a very great temptation to many a man who has a family to feed; besides, there is a propensity in every man to look at what he believes to be nice and tasty, let it be winged game or running. He does not believe, either, that it has been created exclusively for one class of the community; and so he may kill a hare or a rabbit when it passes his way, because his wages are inadequate to meet the demands on them, or from dire necessity, or just because he likes jugged hare as well as anybody else. . . .
>
> I have worked, and I would work, with a man who has been convicted of knocking over a hare or a rabbit, but I should not care to go to work with a man who had taken a hen off a roost. If the poacher was a good workman, it would be all right in my eyes and in the eyes of the other labourers . . . .

> Joseph Arch, *The Story of His Life Told by Himself* (1898), pp.159–63.

5 Conclusion: The Countryside in the Mid-nineteenth Century

The rich man in his castle,
  The poor man at his gate,
God made them high or lowly,
  And ordered their estate.

Mrs C.F. Alexander, *Hymns for Little Children*,
(1848)

Landowners and Clergy

By the middle of the nineteenth century rural society showed many changes compared to its position a century earlier. As a result of enclosure and, in particular, of the post-war agricultural depression the number of small owner-occupiers had dwindled, and the tripartite system of land cultivation, comprising landlord, tenant-farmer and agricultural labourer, had become ever more firmly entrenched. The social repercussions of this were commented upon by a French visitor in the early 1860s:

> At the end of the last century Arthur Young was writing, 'I do not know a single cottage to which a bit of land is not attached.' . . . But by means of 'enclosure acts' the commons have been continuously reduced; thus the peasant can no longer have recourse to his own small supplies of meat, and having sold his strip of land is left with nothing but his two arms, which he now hires out.

Edward Hyams (ed.), *Taine's Notes on England*
(1957), p.133.

144

That was, of course, something of an exaggeration. Even in the 1760s and 1770s many labouring families had been without access either to common land for the grazing of livestock or to small arable plots for the raising of corn and vegetables. But it is undeniable that the number of landless labourers had increased sharply over the period. Only in certain districts, such as Cumbria and the Lincolnshire fens, had owner-cultivators survived on any scale, although most counties had a sprinkling of them. Their pride in their modest independence was captured by William Barnes, when he described a small Dorset freeholder:

> I'm lan'lard o' my little farm,
>   I'm king 'ithin my little pliace;
> I broke noo lā's, I done noo harm,
>   An' bĕnt a'-fear'd o' noo man's fiace.
> When I be cover'd wi' my thatch,
> Noo man da diare to lift my latch;
> Wher honest han's da shut the hatch,
>   There fear da leäve the pliace.

> William Barnes, *Poems of Rural Life in the Dorset
> Dialect*, 'The Huomestead', ll.17-24.

Inevitably the disappearance of men such as he weakened the self-reliance of village communities and confirmed the economic and social pre-eminence of the aristocracy and gentry.

Nevertheless, as Mrs Gaskell has shown, significant differences in prestige could also be identified within these two ruling groups – not merely on financial or property grounds, but for genealogical reasons, too. In *Wives and Daughters* it was Lord and Lady Cumnor who possessed the broadest acres and exercised the greatest power in Hollingford, but it was the bluff Squire Hamley who boasted the longest pedigree and enjoyed the deep local respect which went with it:

> He and his ancestors had been called squire as long back as . . . tradition extended. But there was many a greater landowner in the county, for Squire Hamley's estate

was not more than eight hundred acres or so. But his family had been in possession of it long before the Earls of Cumnor had been heard of; before the Hely-Harrisons had bought Coldstone Park; no one in Hollingford knew the time when the Hamleys had not lived at Hamley. ... But they were not an adventurous race. They never traded, or speculated, or tried agricultural improvements of any kind. They had no capital in any bank; nor what perhaps would have been more in character, hoards of gold in any stocking. Their mode of life was simple, and more like that of yeomen than squires. ... There was a dignity in this quiet conservatism that gained him an immense amount of respect from high and low; and he might have visited at every house in the county had he so chosen. But he was very indifferent to the charms of society ....

> Elizabeth C. Gaskell, *Wives and Daughters* (1866),
> pp.43–44.

Trollope focused upon another aspect of the same question, namely, the important geographical dominance which the larger landowners could achieve in their own locality and which reinforced the authority they exercised:

The squires of Allington had been squires of Allington since squires, such as squires are now, were first known in England. ... The estate of Dale of Allington had been coterminous with the parish of Allington for some hundreds of years; and though ... the race of squires had possessed nothing of superhuman discretion, and had perhaps been guided in their walks through life by no very distinct principles, still ... no acre of the property had ever been parted from the hands of the existing squire. ... At Allington, Dale of Allington had always been known as a king. At Guestwick, the neighbouring market town, he was a great man – to be seen frequently on Saturdays, standing in the market-place, and laying down the law as to barley and oxen among men who knew usually more about barley and oxen than did he. At Hamersham, the assize town, he was generally in some repute, being a constant grand juror for the county, and a man who paid his way. ... Beyond Hamersham [his] fame had not spread itself.

Anthony Trollope, *The Small House at Allington*
(1864), pp.1; 3.

However, if the general leadership role of the major landlords had been reinforced by the partial disappearance of their smaller brethren, their own attitude to their responsibilities had also undergone a change. Partly as a consequence of anxiety at the burgeoning political and economic pretensions of the urban manufacturing and commercial interests and partly due to a greater sense of moral duty induced by the Evangelical Revival within the Anglican Church, they came to regard their duties in a more serious light. Typical of the new order was the 7th Duke of Bedford, who had inherited debts of more than half a million pounds in 1839, but through careful administration had eliminated them by the mid-1850s. During these years he paid close attention not only to raising tillage standards on his estate and improving its general management, but embarked on a major cottage-building programme. He also set in hand various self-help schemes for the villagers. In May 1858 he summarised his general philosophy in a letter to the 7th Duke of Devonshire, who had recently succeeded to the vast Cavendish properties:

The duties and responsibilities of such an estate as yours or mine are very great – we must discharge them as best we can, and make a good amount to look back upon at the close of life – I am pleased to see you paying so much attention to yours – it will afford a fund of satisfaction to others as well as to yourself – and conduce to the well being of those who live upon them.

Quoted in David Spring, *The English Landed Estate in the Nineteenth Century: Its Administration* (1963), p.51.

On another occasion he firmly declared: 'To improve the dwellings of the labouring class, and afford them the means of greater cleanliness, health and comfort, in their own homes . . . are among the first duties and ought to be among the truest pleasures, of every landlord'. (Quoted in Pamela Horn, *The Rural World 1780-1850*, p.229.)

The warm social relationships which could develop where a squire took a personal interest in the welfare of those living upon his estate were described sympathetically by William Barnes:

> An' all the vo'k did love so well
> The good wold squire o' Culver Dell,
> That used to ramble drough the sheädes
> O' timber, or the burnen gleädes,
> An' come at evenen up the leäze
> Wi' red-eär'd dogs bezide his knees,
> An' hold his gun, a-hangen drough
> His eärmpit, out above his tooe,
> Wi' kindly words upon his tongue,
> Vor vo'k that met en, wold an' young,
> Vor he did know the poor so well
> 'S the richest vo'k in Culver Dell.

> William Barnes, 'Culver Dell and the Squire (1859),
> ll.13-24 in *Poems in the Dorset Dialect*, Second
> Collection.

This more caring approach was reflected in the appearance of the countryside too. Estate villages, or 'close' parishes, owned by one or two major landlords only were likely to have better housing and superior amenities – as well as stricter rules and regulations – than those of their 'open' counterparts where ownership was widespread. The resultant physical contrast was noted by Trollope when he compared the modest comfort of Framley with the unattractive nearby open parish of Hogglestock with its brickworks and recalcitrant inhabitants. At Framley there were two schools,

> which owed their erection to Lady Lufton's energy; then came a neat little grocer's shop, the neat grocer

being the clerk and sexton, and the neat grocer's wife the pew-opener in the church. .... At the back of the Court, up one of those cross-roads, there was another small shop or two, and there was a very neat cottage residence, in which lived the widow of a former curate, another protégé of Lady Lufton's; and there was a big, staring, brick house, in which the present curate lived; but this was a full mile distant from the church, and farther from Framley Court, ... Over and above these, there was hardly a house in the parish of Framley, outside the bounds of Framley Court, except those of farmers and farm labourers; and yet the parish was of large extent.

Anthony Trollope, *Framley Parsonage* (1860),
pp.12-13.

The quiet decorum of this estate village differed sharply from the atmosphere in its rougher neighbour. Even Hogglestock's location in the north of Barsetshire had its disadvantages:

Barsetshire, taken altogether, is a pleasant green tree-becrowded county, with large bosky hedges, pretty damp deep lanes, and roads with broad grass margins running along them ... but just up in its northern extremity this nature alters. There it is bleak and ugly, with low artificial hedges and without wood .... There is not a gentleman's house in the parish of Hogglestock besides that of the clergyman; and this, though it is certainly the house of a gentleman, can hardly be said to be fit to be so. It is ugly, and straight, and small. ... And Hogglestock is a large parish. It includes two populous villages, abounding in brickmakers, a race of men very troublesome to a zealous parson who won't let men go rollicking to the devil without interference.

Ibid, pp.153; 155.

Significantly too in England as a whole it was the 'open' villages which predominated throughout the period. They accounted for about four-fifths of all rural parishes in the middle of the nineteenth century, although with sharp regional variations. Whereas over nine-tenths of the townships in Essex, Cambridgeshire and Hertfordshire were open, in Norfolk, Leicestershire, Lincolnshire and the East Riding of Yorkshire the proportion was between a half and two-thirds.

Furthermore, whilst a growing number of landlords conformed to the high standards set by the Duke of Bedford and his fellow 'improvers', not all were either willing or able to undertake the rebuilding, drainage work, fencing and broader social initiatives which such a programme demanded. Some were reluctant to spend the greater part of the year upon their country estates and preferred instead to devote time and money to gambling, horse racing and the pursuit of pleasure, as their predecessors of the Regency era had done. The poor financial returns to be derived from landed property in the mid-century as compared to the period of high prices and enclosure fifty years earlier added to their disillusion. 'What an infernal bore is landed property', commented Lord Monson sourly in 1851. 'No certain income can be reckoned upon. I hope your future wife will have Consols or some such ballast, I think it is worth half as much again as what land is reckoned at.' Even Sir James Graham, owner of 26 000 acres at Netherby, Cumberland, and an enthusiastic improver, was forced to admit gloomily in 1845: 'I cannot endure this state of affairs, which oppresses me, and which renders all my possessions grievous to me instead of pleasurable'. The immediate cause of his concern was a heavy debt which he had incurred partly through carrying out work on the estate. In other cases, however, debts were contracted for less worthy motives, as the Duke of Wellington critically observed of certain of his own relatives:

> I am sorry to learn that the Duke of Buckingham's Affairs are likely to turn out so ill. It is unpardonable in a man of great family to get into such difficulties; and more so in this family than in any other. This one, his father, and grandfather married heiresses . . . and other branches of the family have married heiresses!
> My nephew the Duke of Beaufort is in a bad way! He

I understand had . . . put down his establishments and gone abroad, to pass the Winter in Italy. He is married to my Niece!

Then my Nephew the Earl of Mornington has ruined several estates. His first wife had not less than £50,000 a year! She left two sons. Their estate is totally destroyed and gone . . . .

They all face establishments larger than they can maintain! Then they indulge themselves in every fancy . . . always fancying that their whole fortune is at their disposal . . . forgetting their expensive establishments and other charges . . . .

Quoted in Clara Burdett Patterson, *Angela Burdett-Coutts and the Victorians* (1953), pp.103-104. (The Duke was writing on 18 September 1847.)

In the event the Duke of Buckingham went bankrupt in 1848 with debts of £1.5 million, most of them incurred by heavy expenditure on rebuilding his estate at Stowe and on various political campaigns. But such men as he were already becoming anachronisms in early Victorian England, survivors from an older, more reckless era.

As in the eighteenth century, the larger estates also continued to exert an important influence upon local employment. Of Woburn, the Duke of Bedford's principal seat, Lord Shaftesbury commented: 'It is not a palace, a house; it is a town, a municipal borough, a city'. Apart from indoor staff, who might number from six or eight servants in the smaller households to forty or fifty in the larger, there was a wide range of outdoor workers. These included gardeners, builders, carpenters and other craftsmen employed to maintain estate buildings, as well as a bailiff, foremen and labourers deployed on the home farm, and keepers engaged about the game preserves. Thus a comparatively modest property – Shrubland Hall in Suffolk – had a mid-century staff of 173. Among them were 17 indoor servants, 16 in the stables, 40 gardeners, 38 men on the home farm, 16 keepers and night men, 4 warreners, 7 carpenters, 9 engaged in the brick kilns and 2 blacksmiths.

The greater sense of responsibility displayed by many of the larger landowners was matched by a similar concern on the part of the rising generation of clergy. The days of the hard-drinking, hard-riding, non-resident cleric were virtually at an end. More characteristic of the new breed were men like William Andrew, then incumbent of Ketteringham, Norfolk, who combined zeal in charitable works – including the dispensing of medicines – with deep religious convictions, as entries in his diary make clear. Thus on 4 December 1840 he wrote:

> The effect of my new medicine is astonishing! Thirling two years ago was at the brink of the grave and has had another attack of liver complaint. I began with brandy and salt, which at first produced a kind of intoxicated feeling, with increased headache and a warm glow through the whole frame. She persisted according to my prescribed plan, first rubbing the crown with about a tablespoonful and then the first thing in the morning taking internally the same quantity with double quantity of boiling water. She is much better. ... She is very grateful. May it be an open door for me to her soul. Lord, leave not her soul unhealed!
>
> Quoted in Owen Chadwick, *Victorian Miniature* (1960), p.53.

Perhaps the clearest summary of the changes which had taken place was provided by Alfred Blomfield, son of Bishop Charles Blomfield. He compared mid-century attitudes with those when his father began his ministry:

> In character, habits, attainments, social position, and general reputation, the ordinary clergyman of 1860 is a very different being from the clergyman of 1810 . . . .
> The most obvious difference is the low standard of character and duties which then prevailed among clergymen compared to what is now generally expected of them. Fifty years ago, a decent and regular performance of Divine Service on Sundays was almost all that any one looked for in a clergyman: if this were

found, most people were satisfied. The clergyman might be non-resident, a sportsman, a farmer, neglectful of all study, a violent politician, a *bon vivant*, or a courtier; but if he performed in person, or by deputy, that which now usurped the name of his "duty," that was enough . . . .

The natural consequence of this state of things was a very low standard of theological acquirements among the country clergy. When they were useful and well-informed they busied themselves generally with matters foreign to their own profession. They were eager politicians, or amateur farmers; they were "constant readers of the Gentleman's Magazine, deep in the antiquities of the signs of inns, speculations as to what becomes of swallows in winter, and whether hedgehogs, or other urchins, are most justly accused of sucking milch cows dry at night." . . .

The Bishops, though numbering some men of superior stamp among them, and as a body decorous in private character, were often either politically subservient, avaricious, courtiers, domineering, or neglectful of their dioceses. Indeed, measured by the standard of our own days, even the best would be considered as deficient in some parts of his office. Bishop Porteus (1776-1808) was justly honoured as an amiable and conscientious prelate; yet, when asked by a neighbouring clergyman to preach a charity sermon for him, he could reply, "I only give one in a year, and *the next year is promised.*"

Alfred Blomfield (ed.), *A Memoir of Charles James Blomfield* (1863), Vol. I, pp.56–61.

Significantly, Bishop Blomfield, shortly after moving to the diocese of London, had made clear his own reformist stance on these issues. In a letter to one of his clerics in April 1839 he firmly declared:

I have more than once told the clergy in general, and I have still more pointedly told those whom I have myself ordained, that no hunting clergyman can ever be an efficient minister of religion. The pursuit is utterly inconsistent with that seriousness and quietness of demeanour and conduct, the want of which must weaken, if it does not destroy, the effect of his preaching. The pretext of health I consider to be wholly inadmissable. A clergyman may take horse exercise without hunting; and although hunting with beagles is less boisterous and unseemly than other kinds of hunting, still it *is* hunting, and in your own case it is felt to be inconsistent with what is due to the clerical office . . . .

Ibid, Vol. II, pp.200-201.

Farmers

As in the late eighteenth century, so in the middle of the nineteenth, agricultural improvement became an issue of growing interest for many landowners. Some took a personal interest in livestock breeding or in the organising of model farms, while others supported the agricultural societies which were growing up to spread these new ideas. Sir James Graham and his agent, for example, organised the Netherby tenants into a farmers' society, with a special cattle show held each year at which prizes were offered. And on the national stage owners like Earl Spencer took an active part in promoting the Royal Agricultural Society when this was formed at the end of the 1830s.

In applying 'improved' farming methods to individual holdings, however, much depended upon the tenant himself. By the mid-1850s it was noted that tenant farmers had taken over from the major proprietors as the principal purchasers of agricultural machinery, while it was they who were trying out the growing variety of fertilisers which were coming on the market.

But the farming class of early Victorian England showed wide variations, both on a geographical basis – with the preoccupations of pastoral producers having little in common with those of the cereal men – and in the size of the holdings they cultivated and the methods they employed. As James Caird commented:

> To show the progress which has been made in the art of agriculture in this country, it is not necessary to go back to any authority of the last century for a description of the processes then adopted. Every county presents contrasts abundantly instructive, the most antiquated and the most modern systems being found side by side. The successful practices of one farm, or one county, are unknown or unheeded in the next. On one side of a hedge a plough with five horses and two men, and on the other side of the same hedge, a plough with two horses and one man, are doing precisely the same amount of work. . . . On neighbouring farms of similar soil the wheat crop may vary from twenty to forty bushels an acre, and most probably the man who grows twenty pays not less than 9s. for thrashing that quantity by hand, while the other thrashes his forty bushels by steam for 3s. 6d.
>
> James Caird, *English Agriculture in 1850-51* (1852), pp.498-99.

Lack of education, inadequate capital and innate conservatism were the prime reasons why some men clung to the old ways when new, improved ones were available. R.S. Surtees, as a practical agriculturalist, was particularly scathing in his condemnation of the small cultivators of Durham, where his own estate was situated. He described Henerey Brown, a typical example of that despised breed, who excused a failure to pay his rent on audit day by blaming everything but his own inefficiency:

> 'The land's far worse nor we took it for – some of the plough's a shem to be seen – wor stable rains in desprate – there isn't a dry place for a coo – the back wall of the barn's all bulgin oot – the pigs get into wor garden for want of a gate – there isn't a fence 'ill turn a foal – the

hars eat all wor tormots – we're perfectly ruined wi' rats,' and altogether Henerey opened such a battery of grievances as completely drove Sir Moses, [his landlord] . . . from his seat, and made him leave the finish of his friend to Mr. Teaser [the agent]. . . .

Mr. Teaser then proceeded with the wretched audit, each succeeding tenant being a repetition of the first – excuses – drawbacks – allowances for lime – money no matter to Sir Moses – and this with a whole year's rent due, to say nothing of hopeless arrears.

R.S. Surtees, *Ask Mamma* (1858), p.213.

Much the same applied to South Lancashire, where Caird noted that, although consumers had increased rapidly in the wake of industrial development, yet the level of farming lagged behind. 'Unfortunately the great proportion of the country is held by small farmers who, however industrious, do not possess the intelligence or capital requisite to meet the natural difficulties . . ., while much of it being held on life leases, and the great proportion of the rest on tenures from year to year, there is wanting, also, that permanent interest in the land which forms the chief motive to an improving farmer.' (James Caird, *English Agriculture in 1850-51* (1852), p.265.) Nevertheless, efficient men were to be found:

The farm of Mr. Neilson, of Halewood, exhibits several points worthy of notice. A light tramway with waggons is made use of for taking the turnip crop off the ground in moist weather. The tramway is readily shifted, and the crop is thrown into the waggons, which are then each pushed along by a man, so that the entire crop may be removed from the ground, which thus receives no injury from the feet of horses. The tramway can be constructed for 1s. 4d. per yard, and might be very advantageously introduced on all heavy farms where it is found difficult to take off the turnip crop in moist weather. A gang of men are at present employed on a considerable field of Mr. Neilson's in taking off the turnip crop, which they draw from the ground, fill into

the waggons, and convey outside of the gate at the rate
of 6s. an acre, shifting the tramway at their own cost. At
this work they earn 2s. 3d. a day. A large stock of dairy
cows is kept on this farm.

James Caird, *English Agriculture in 1850-51* (1852),
pp.270-71.

It was that businesslike approach to agriculture which
Tennyson also had in mind for his veteran Northern farmer:

Dubbut looök at the waäste: theer warn't not feeäd for a
cow;
Nowt at all but bracken an' fuzz, an' looök at it now –
Warnt worth nowt a haäcre, an' now theer's lots o'
feeäd,
Fourscoor yows upon it an' some on it down i' seeäd.

Nobbut a bit on it's left, an' I meäned to 'a stubbed it at
fall,
Done it ta-year I meäned, an' runned plow thruff it an'
all,
If godamoighty an' parson 'ud nobbut let ma aloän,
Meä, wi haäte hoonderd haäcre o' Squoire's, an' lond o'
my oän.

Alfred Tennyson, *Northern Farmer: Old Style*
(1864), ll.37-44.

But one of the clearest indications of the changes in
community life which could follow upon 'improvement' was
given by William Dickinson in a survey of East Cumberland.
He contrasted the penny-pinching conditions of the pre-
enclosure era with the position in the 1850s:

In those days the chief dependence of the small farmer
was on the commons. They ploughed little, and
whether one or more horses were kept, they were
invariably turned on the common to *exist*, . . .
whenever their services were not required on the
farm . . . . The flock of geese, from April till the

stubbles were ready, were always kept on the common. The pigs were driven out daily in summer to 'fend' as they best could. Even the milk cows were obliged to be turned out whenever the in-field pasture grew bare . . . . The children of the farmers and cottagers also were employed nearly half the summer on the moors gathering cranberries and bleaberries in the season, and rushes for winter lights – drying peats, &c. But all this was . . . only a small portion of the services the commons were expected and compelled to perform. Their main use was in maintaining flocks of sheep for the adjoining occupiers . . . . During the forty years, from about 1780 to 1820, Acts of Parliament were obtained for enclosing and dividing the greater part of the numerous commons; and then commenced that series of alterations . . ., and improvements in . . . agriculture . . . . Meadows began to appear where swamps existed before; plantations dotted the country where heather and whins had formerly been; new farm-buildings were erected, and old ones renewed; straight fences were seen in direct contrast with the zig-zag hedges of the ancient inclosures; the varied stages of cultivation diversified and improved the aspect of the whole country; the area of arable land was nearly, if not fully, doubled in extent; and along with all these changes the habits of the people were converted from the listless lounge of the half-shepherd, half-husbandman, to the active, industrious, and persevering qualities of the agriculturist, who has now been taught to feel that the welfare of himself and family must depend entirely on his own energies . . . . In former times nearly all the wearing apparel of the country people went through the various stages of its manufacture in the retired villages or cottages attached to the farms. The woollen clothing and bedding required in the country was teased, carded, and spun by the farmers' families in the winter evenings (the men assisting); and was woven, fulled, dyed, and walked by village hand-loom weavers, fullers, dyers, and walkers, and made up by village tailors; – the remainder of the wool produced on the small farms was spun at home, and sold in the market-towns by the farmers' wives and cottagers.

A portion of lint, or line-seed, was then grown on nearly every farm, and its conversion into hand-made thread was likewise a winter's evening's occupation on the farms; . . . . Now, nearly all the various craftsmen employed on these fabrics reside in towns, and the rural population is more exclusively agricultural. The villages generally consist of farmers' houses, cottages for labourers, and an artisan or two of each class required in the manufacture of farm implements and repairs, with a few shops . . . . The household duties are multiplied and different from those of former times, and leave less leisure for such occupations as our ancestors spent their evenings with. The female members of the family now generally ply the needle, either in knitting or sewing, while the master and his sons have accounts to make up, either relating to some parochial office, or their private affairs.

Commonly, a newspaper finds its way into every farm-house, with one or more of the numerous periodicals of the day, and thus, by slow but sure gradations, the whole routine of nearly every farmer's household is utterly changed.

William Dickinson, *Essay on the Agriculture of East Cumberland* (1853), pp.9–12.

Rural Tradesmen and Labourers

Throughout the years from the 1760s to the 1850s rural tradesmen and women played a vital role in promoting the smooth running of community life and in adding to its social diversity. The 'leavening' influence they exerted can be gauged from an examination of the 1851 Population Census returns. Thus at Wyverstone, Suffolk, out of 114 males employed in the village at that date 15 were farmers or their sons, 77 were agricultural workers and 17 were tradespeople of various kinds. They included 4 blacksmiths and their apprentices, 6 shoemakers, a tailor, a miller, a butcher and a grocer. And among the women, of 24 with specific occupations, 2 were dressmakers and 2 shoebinders, 19 were domestic servants or dairymaids and 1 was a teacher.

Even at this date many retailing attitudes were unashamedly conservative and it was only after the construction of the railways and the resultant broadening of trading links that methods began to change. A more profit-conscious spirit slowly took possession of shopkeepers and customers alike, with the latter beginning to look for low prices or more attractive merchandise, rather than merely continuing to patronise the place where they and their family had done business in the past. This transition in marketing ideas was identified by George Eliot:

> Grimworth, to a discerning eye, was a good place to set up shopkeeping in. There was no competition in it at present; the Church-people had their own grocer and draper; the Dissenters had theirs, and the two or three butchers found a ready market for their joints without strict reference to religious persuasion . . . .
>
> The shopkeepers at Grimworth were by no means unanimous as to the advantages promised by [the] prospect of increased population and trading, being substantial men, who liked doing a quiet business in which they were sure of their customers, and could calculate their returns to a nicety. Hitherto, it had been held a point of honour by the families in Grimworth parish, to buy their sugar and their flannel at the shops where their fathers and mothers had bought before them; but, if new-comers were to bring in the system of neck-and-neck trading, and solicit feminine eyes by gown-pieces laid in fan-like folds, and surmounted by artificial flowers, giving them a factitious charm (for on what human figure would a gown sit like a fan, or what female head was like a bunch of China-asters?), or, if new grocers were to fill their windows with mountains of currants and sugar, made seductive by contrast and tickets, – what security was there for Grimworth, that a vagrant spirit in shopping,

once introduced, would not in the end carry the most important families to the larger market town of Cattleton, where, business being done on a system of small profits and quick returns, the fashions were of the freshest, and goods of all kinds might be bought at an advantage?

George Eliot, *Brother Jacob* (1860), pp.494-96.

To many old-style country tradesmen, therefore, the growing importance of mass-produced goods from urban factories and the changes in business methods which accompanied their introduction posed an unwelcome threat. Their difficulties were compounded by the fact that as a result of enclosure a number of those who had combined work on a small plot of land with the pursuit of a craft or trade, were now driven to rely upon their trade alone. At Bere Regis (Dorset) the nineteen carpenters recorded in the parish in 1841 included several families who had entered the trade because they had lost their small holdings, and carpentry was a craft of which most small farmers had a knowledge (Barbara Kerr, *Bound to the Soil* (1968), p.133). Some men reacted by altering their own business methods to move with the times. Blacksmiths, for example, began to abandon machine-making and concentrated on repairs instead. But others neglected to take any positive action and experienced growing difficulties. The shrinkage in the number of tradesmen which resulted, affected the overall quality of community life, for they were always likely to be more independent in their attitudes than were the agricultural labourers. The radicalness of the village shoemaker was proverbial, and it is significant that, when Alton Locke went out on his political campaign among the rural labourers, it was with a cobbler that he stayed: 'He took me into his little cabin, and there, with the assistance of a shrewd, good-natured wife, shared with me the best he had; and after supper commenced, mysteriously and in trembling, as if the very walls might have ears, a rambling, bitter diatribe on the wrongs and sufferings of the labourers . . . .' (Charles Kingsley, *Alton Locke* (1850), pp.247-48.) It is to the position of the village labourer that we must now turn.

By the 1850s the living standards of most workers had

clearly improved compared to the deep distress and privation they had endured during the French War period and its immediate aftermath. Nevertheless, particularly in the southern and south Midland counties, much still remained to be done. As James Caird noted, whilst the highest rate of pay he had encountered on his 1850-51 tour of England was the 15s. per week secured in parts of Lancashire, within south Wiltshire basic rates of as little as 6s. a week were payable. He attributed the higher earnings in the northern counties to 'the proximity of manufacturing and mining enterprise', adding sharply:

> The influence of manufacturing enterprise is thus seen to add 37 per cent. to the wages of the agricultural labourers of the Northern counties, as compared with those of the South. The line is distinctly drawn at the point where coal ceases to be found, to the south of which there is only one of the counties we visited in which the wages reach 10s. a week, Sussex. The local circumstances of that county explain the cause of labour being there better remunerated; the wealthy population of Brighton, and other places on the Sussex coast, affording an increased market for labour beyond the demands of agriculture.
>
> A comparison with the price of labour in the same counties in 1770 will show this influence clearly. In Cumberland, at that time, the wages of the agricultural labourer were 6s. 6d., in the West Riding 6s., in Lancashire 6s. 6d.; in each of which counties they have since increased fully 100 per cent. . . . The increase in the eighteen Southern counties . . . is under 14 per cent. In some of them there is no increase whatever, the wages of the agricultural labourer in part of Berkshire and Wilts. being precisely the same as they were 80 years ago, and in Suffolk absolutely less. . . .
>
> Nothing could show more unequivocally the advantage of manufacturing enterprise to the prosperity and advancement of the farm-labourer.

> James Caird *English Agriculture in 1850-51* (1852),
> pp.511-12.

Although employment on railway construction in the 1840s and 1850s offered some opportunities for labourers to earn better wages in the southern and south-Midland counties, the number of vacancies for navvies was always limited. More significant was the willingness of men to leave the villages to seek work in urban trades or the mining industry of the North and Wales. In the rural Midlands population-falls first became apparent in parishes contiguous to the main line of the London and North-Western Railway, and as early as 1836 there were claims that the migration opportunities offered by the railways had brought full employment to south-west Bedfordshire. Overall, the number of agricultural labourers, shepherds and farm servants employed in England and Wales fell by just over one per cent in the 1850s – a total of around twelve thousand men. In the decades which lay ahead that process was speeded up and these migrants were joined by many thousand more.

But even where advances were achieved in rural living standards, countless families still experienced great difficulties in making ends meet. Children were sent out to work as early as possible to help eke out a scanty parental income, and Charles Kingsley, as a Christian Socialist, bitterly contrasted the comfortable conditions enjoyed by the livestock upon 'improved' farms with the ragged, ill-fed youngsters sent to tend them:

> We trudged on, over wide stubbles, with innumerable weeds; over wide fallows, in which the deserted ploughs stood frozen fast; ... then over a field of turnips, where we passed a large fold of hurdles, within which some hundred sheep stood, with their heads turned from the cutting blast. ... As we came up to the fold, two little boys hailed us from the inside – two little wretches with blue noses and white cheeks, scarecrows of rags and patches, their feet peeping through bursten shoes twice too big for them, who seemed to have shared between them a ragged pair of worsted gloves, and cowered among the sheep, under the shelter of a hurdle, crying and inarticulate with cold.
> 'What's the matter, boys?'
> 'Turmits is froze, and us can't turn the handle of the cutter. Do ye gie us a turn, please?'

We scrambled over the hurdles, and gave the miserable little creatures the benefit of ten minutes' labour. They seemed too small for such exertion: their little hands were purple with chilblains, and they were so sorefooted they could scarcely limp. I was surprised to find them at least three years older than their size and looks denoted, and still more surprised, too, to find that their salary for all this bitter exposure to the elements ... was the vast sum of one shilling a week each, Sundays included. 'They didn't never go to school, nor to church nether, except just now and then, sometimes – they had to mind the shep.'

I went on, sickened with the contrast between the highly-bred, over-fed, fat, thick-woolled animals, with their troughs of turnips and malt-dust, and their racks of rich clover-hay, and their little pent-house of rock-salt, having nothing to do but to eat and sleep, and eat again, and the little half-starved shivering animals who were their slaves.

Charles Kingsley, *Alton Locke* (1850), p.249.

Even the French visitor, Taine, although generally favourable to the improved farming he saw, could not forbear to comment upon the poor condition of houses he visited in villages about thirty to forty miles from London – or upon the zeal of housewives in keeping their small dwellings neat and tidy:

Some of the cottages are very poor, built of wattle and daub (*pisé*), with thatched roofs, the rooms too low and too small, the windows also too small, the interior walls too thin. Think of a large family crowded into two such rooms in winter, with clothes drying on them, baby linen hung up to air, and a roaring fire: during the long periods of rain and snow, they must live in an unwholesome atmosphere, breathing their own bodily emanations.

Many of the mothers have haggard faces blotchily red, and a wasted, exhausted look; they have too many children and are all overtired. The tenant of one of these cottages was a day-labourer, married, father of six children, and earning twelve shillings a week. He is usually taken on by the year or half-year. A cottage like his costs between three and four pounds a year. His face was drawn, strained, sad and humble . . . .

However, his little house was clean: the blue-patterned plates were ranged in good order above a dresser. The iron fireplace was tidy. I had already seen cottages of this class elsewhere; almost always, at least in one room, there is an old carpet on the floor. There is often wall-paper, chairs of well-polished wood; small, framed prints; always a Bible and sometimes a few other books – works of piety, modern novels, how to rear rabbits, and so forth. . . . The floors are well-swept, nothing is left lying about.

> Edward Hyams (ed.), *Taine's Notes on England*
> (1957), pp.128-29.

But another foreign traveller, the American farmer, Frederick Olmsted, drew attention to another, less desirable, aspect of labouring life. That was the widespread practice of supplying alcohol as part of the men's remuneration instead of their being paid wholly in cash. In Olmsted's view this encouraged drunkenness. Indeed, used as he was to the freer social climate and the greater prosperity of his homeland, his conclusions were more pessimistic than those of Taine. He was especially critical of the ignorance and lack of 'intelligence' which seemed characteristic of labourers in the west of England. Thus in Warminster he got into conversation with three smock-frocked workers whom he met in a taproom, but soon found he must abandon the effort:

I could make nothing of two-thirds of their replies, and I doubted if they could understand me much better. So I contented myself with listening, while they continued to talk or mumble with each other. The subjects of their conversation were beer and 'the girls:' of the latter topic they said nothing to be repeated; of the former, they wished the farmers never gave worse drink than that they were now enjoying – 'it was most good for nothing, some of it, what they gave out.' And one told how he had had to drink so much of it once, it had made him clear sick; . . . .

> Frederick Law Olmsted, *Walks and Talks of An American Farmer in England* (1967), pp.253-54. (Olmsted visited England in 1850.)

Similarly of an encounter in Herefordshire during June 1850 he gloomily declared:

Our guide was a man of about forty, having a wife and seven children; neither he nor any of his family (he thought) could read or write, and, except with regard to his occupation as agricultural laborer, I scarcely ever saw a man of so limited information . . . . His wages were seven shillings – sometimes had been eight – a week . . . . It was a common thing that they had nothing to eat but dry bread. . . . In addition to his wages, the master gave him, as he did all the laborers, three quarts either of cider or beer a day, sometimes one and sometimes the other. He liked cider best – thought there was 'more strength to it.' Harvest-time they got six quarts, and sometimes, when the work was very hard, he had ten quarts. . . . A working-man must have zider or beer – there was no use to argue against that. That 'Jesus Christ came into the world to save sinners,' and that 'work without beer is death,' was the alpha and omega of his faith.

The laborers in this part of England (Hereford, Monmouth, Gloucester, and Wiltshire) were the most degraded, poor, stupid, brutal, and licentious that we saw in the kingdom. . . . I did not see in Ireland, or in Germany or in France, nor did I ever see among our negroes or Indians, or among the Chinese or Malays, men whose tastes were such mere instincts, or whose purpose of life and whose mode of life was so low, so like that of domestic animals altogether, as these farm-laborers.

Ibid, pp.236-39.

Doubtless Olmsted's unfamiliar accent and his probing questions confused the uneducated, inarticulate labourers whom he met. But even when allowance is made for this, the picture he paints is a depressing one.

Rural England, then, in the 1850s as in the 1760s, was an unequal society, the lower orders of which were kept firmly under the paternalistic influence of the nobility and gentry. Although in national affairs the power of the landed interest was beginning to wane, within the countryside it faced little challenge, despite the changes which had taken place. As David Spring has written:

At bottom it was not the pursuit of profit that informed the agricultural enterprise of a great English landed estate. Instead what moved it was the spirit of a traditional and hierarchical society led by the landed gentlemen of the nation. So long as that society was vital, so long as the owners of estates were accepted as England's rulers, landlords would show the persistence and ingenuity of Sir James Graham in his reform of Netherby's farming. . . . It was altogether fitting that tenants, agent, and landlord assemble in death as in life in the little churchyard of Arthuret, their tombs so placed as to indicate station and rank; the squire and his family set apart, their burial stones as simple as any; the agent a bit aloof from the cluster of tenants, but all suggesting nevertheless a unity of outlook and purpose.

David Spring, 'A Great Agricultural Estate:
Netherby under Sir James Graham, 1820-1845'
in *Agricultural History*, Vol. 29 (1955),
p.81.

Significantly, as late as 1863 Richard Cobden, the Anti-Corn Law leader and a major industrialist, could condemn the anxiety of well-to-do professional men, merchants and manufacturers to ape the life-style of the landed gentry. Many sent their sons to the newly reformed public schools where they absorbed the same moral values, religious beliefs and classical education as the sons of the gentry with whom they mixed. 'We have the spirit of feudalism rife and rampant in the midst of the antagonistic development of the age of Watt, Arkwright and Stephenson', Cobden declared. 'Manufacturers and merchants as a rule seem only to desire riches that they may be able to prostrate themselves at the feet of feudalism.' (Quoted in Lawrence Stone and Jeanne C. Fawtier Stone, *An Open Elite? England 1540-1880* (1984), p.27.) Coming from such a source, it was a powerful tribute to the ability of the landed elite to retain their authority and prestige well into the second half of the nineteenth century.

Chronological Table

Social history by its very nature is concerned more with processes than events. Thus the enclosure movement and the building of canals, turnpike roads and railways proceeded over long years within the period 1760-1850s. But specific dates and events provide important signposts along the route of these broader changes.

Date	Contemporary events	Publications
1759	The Bridgewater Canal constructed. Over the next 60 years 2200 miles of still water and 2000 miles of river navigation opened	
1768		Arthur Young, *A Six Weeks' Tour through the Southern Counties*
1769		Arthur Young, *A Six Months' Tour through the North of England*
1770		Oliver Goldsmith, *The Deserted Village*; Arthur Young, *Rural Economy; or Essays on the Practical Parts of Husbandry*
1776		Adam Smith, *The Wealth of Nations*
c.1776-77	First annual sheep-shearing fair at Holkham (Norfolk); Thomas Coke of Holkham practised the 'Norfolk System' of large farms, long leases and crop rotations	
1777	Foundation of the Bath and West Agricultural Society	
1780	c.40% of labour force engaged in agriculture	
1781	James Watt patented the rotary steam-engine	

Date	Contemporary events	Publications
1782	Gilbert's Act (permitting parishes to use workhouses merely for the aged, poor and infirm and not as a place of punishment). By 1830 only about 1000 out of 15 000 parishes had availed themselves of this power	
1783	Lancelot ('Capability') Brown died	George Crabbe, *The Village*
1785	Meikle's threshing machine	William Cowper, *The Task*
1787	Wilberforce began parliamentary campaign against the slave trade	William Marshall, *The Rural Economy of Norfolk*
1791	London Veterinary College established	
1793	Outbreak of war with France; lasted with one short break until 1815. Accelerated Enclosure Movement (2000 Acts in this period). Board of Agriculture founded; it lasted until 1822	
1795	Bad harvests and food riots; Speenhamland system of Poor Relief	David Davies, *The Case of Labourers in Husbandry*
1798	The Smithfield Club inaugurated	T.R. Malthus, *Essay on the Principle of Population*; Sir Frederic Eden, *The State of the Poor*
1799	First patent for a reaping machine issued to Joseph Bryce of London	
1800		Robert Bloomfield, *The Farmer's Boy*
1801	First General Enclosure Act; first decennial Census of England and Wales (population 9 million – 18 million in 1851)	
1803	Ellenborough's Act (poachers offering armed resistance to lawful arrest might be hanged)	Humphry Repton, *The Theory and Practice of Landscape Gardening*

Date	Contemporary events	Publications
1806		Humphry Repton, *An Inquiry into the Changes of Taste in Landscape Gardening*
1807		George Crabbe, *The Parish Register*
1810	c.33% of labour force engaged in agriculture	George Crabbe, *The Borough*
1811	The National Society (for Promoting the Education of the Poor in the Principles of the Established Church) founded	
1814	The British and Foreign School Society formed to provide education for Protestant children of all denominations	Jane Austen, *Mansfield Park*
1815	Battle of Waterloo; end of Napoleonic Wars; Corn Law passed restricting sale of foreign grain until domestic price had reached a particular level (wheat 80s. a quarter). Ineffective and controversial. Amended in 1820s	Jane Austen, *Emma*
1816	Game Law passed (possession of poaching equipment by night subject to seven years' transportation); agricultural riots in East Anglia	
1817-19	Economic recession; poor relief at £8 million per annum (1783 – less than £2m; 1815-16 £5.7m)	
1819	Peterloo 'Massacre'	
1820		John Clare, *Poems Descriptive of Rural Life*
1821	Report from the Committee on the Depressed State of Agriculture in the United Kingdom, Parl. Papers, 1821, Vol. 9 (average wages 9-10s. per week – in 1814 12-15s.)	John Clare, *The Village Minstrel and other poems*; William Cobbett began *Rural Rides*

Date	Contemporary events	Publications
1822	Machine-breaking in Norfolk	
1824		Mary Russell Mitford had first volume of *Our Village* published
1827	Mantraps and spring guns prohibited for use in preserving game	
1828	Night Poaching Act passed (maximum sentence 3 months' hard labour with subsequent personal surety of £10 and two others of £5 each: transportation only for a third offence)	
1830	'Swing' riots in southern and south-midland counties among destitute agricultural labourers; first steam-engine for drainage purposes (installed at Weston Zoyland); opening of the Liverpool and Manchester Railway	William Cobbett completed *Rural Rides*
1831	Archaic qualifications to shoot game abolished; penalties for poaching relaxed	
1832	Reform Act passed	
1833	First government grant for elementary education (£20 000)	
1834	Poor Law Amendment Act; 'Tolpuddle Martyrs' – 6 Dorset labourers sentenced to transportation for administering unlawful oaths in connection with illegal societies (allowed to return to England after c.3 years)	
1835	Introduction of guano as fertiliser from Peru	John Clare, *The Rural Muse*
1836	Tithe Commutation Act (cash system replaced payment in kind)	

Date	Contemporary events	Publications
1838	Foundation of the English Agricultural Society (in 1840 the Royal Agricultural Society of England); Anti-Corn-Law League established to agitate for free trade	R.S. Surtees, *Jorrocks' Jaunts and Jollities* (originally in *New Sporting Magazine*, 1831-34)
1839	First Royal Agricultural Society Show; use of mobile steam-engines in agriculture; County Police Act permitted magistrates at quarter sessions to establish a police force in county areas. Only about half the counties of England and Wales had adopted the measure before county forces were made obligatory in 1856	
1842	Superphosphate factory at Deptford; Lawes and Gilbert's experiments at Rothamsted led to use of inorganic fertilisers	Charles Apperley ('Nimrod'), *The Life of a Sportsman*
1843	Select Committee on Allotments	R.S. Surtees, *Handley Cross* (expanded, 1854)
1844	The Royal College of Veterinary Surgeons founded	William Barnes, *Poems of Rural Life in the Dorset Dialect*
1845	The Royal Agricultural College, Cirencester, established	
1845-47	'Railway mania' (2440 miles of track in 1845; 6080 in 1850) made possible the large-scale movement of livestock for the first time, other than on foot	
1846	Repeal of the Corn Laws	
1851	Census: 1 788 000 men and 229 000 women in agriculture, horticulture and forestry (21.5% of labour force); The Great Exhibition at Crystal Palace (Hussey's and	Charles Kingsley, *Yeast*; James Caird, *English Agriculture in 1850-51*

Date	Contemporary events	Publications
1851 – *contd*	McCormick's American reapers shown to the British public at the Exhibition; forerunners of a new era of harvesting technology); Fowler's drainage apparatus for pipe-laying utilised	
1851-56	Development of steam-powered cultivators	
1853		R.S. Surtees, *Mr. Sponge's Sporting Tour*
1856	Fowler's patent for ploughing with two traction engines	
1859		George Eliot, *Adam Bede*

Bibliography

Primary Sources

Agricultural State of the Kingdom in February, March and April 1816, The (London, 1816)

Andrews, C. Bruyn and Andrews Fanny (eds), *The Torrington Diaries* (London, 1954)

Arch, Joseph, *The Story of His Life Told by Himself* (London, 1898)

Austen, Jane, *Emma* (London, 1971)

——, *Letters of*, ed. R.W. Chapman, 2nd edn (London, 1952)

——, *Mansfield Park* (London, 1970)

——, *Pride and Prejudice* (London, 1970)

——, *Sanditon* (Harmondsworth, 1974)

Barnes, William, *Poems of Rural Life in the Dorset Dialect* (London, 1847)

——, *The Poems of William Barnes*, 2 vols (London, 1962)

Blomfield, Alfred (ed.), *A Memoir of Charles James Blomfield*, 2 vols, (London, 1863)

Bloomfield, Robert, MSS at the British Library, Add. MSS 28, 268

——, *The Farmer's Boy* (Lavenham, 1971)

Borrow, George, *Lavengro* (Oxford, 1982)

Britton, John, *The Autobiography of*, 3 parts (London, 1850)

Brontë, Charlotte, *Jane Eyre* (London, 1973)

Brontë, Emily, *Wuthering Heights* (Harmondsworth, 1984)

Buckmaster, John, *A Village Politician* (Horsham, 1982)

Butler, E.M. (ed.), *A Regency Visitor: The English Tour of Prince Pückler-Muskau, 1826-1828* (London, 1957)

Byron, Lord, *The Age of Bronze* in *The Poetical Works of Lord Byron*, 6 vols (London, 1855-56)

Caird, James, *English Agriculture in 1850-51* (London, 1852)

Chadwick, Owen, *Victorian Miniature* (London, 1960)

Clare, John, *The Poems of John Clare*, ed. J.W. Tibble, 2 vols (London, 1935)

——, *The Prose of John Clare*, eds J.W. and Anne Tibble (London, 1951)

Cobbett, William, *Autobiography of*, ed. W. Reitzel (London, 1967)

Cobbett's Political Register (November and December 1830)

——, *Rural Rides*, 2 vols, Everyman's Library (London, 1948)

Constabulary Force, Report of Royal Commission on, Parliamentary Papers, 1839, Vol. XIX

Cowper, William, *The Task* (1785) in *Cowper: Poetical Works*, ed. H.S. Milford, 4th edn (London, 1967)

Crabbe, George, *Poems*, ed. Adolphus W. Ward, 3 vols (Cambridge, 1907)

Cuming, E.D. (ed.), *Town and Country Papers by Robert Smith Surtees* (London and Edinburgh, 1929)

Davies, David, *The Case of Labourers in Husbandry Stated and Considered* (London, 1795)

Dickinson, William, *Essay on the Agriculture of East Cumberland* (Carlisle, 1853)

Disraeli, Benjamin, *Coningsby* (Harmondsworth, 1983)

——, *Sybil or: The Two Nations* (Harmondsworth, 1954)

Dyer, John, *Poems of* (London: T. Fisher Unwin, n.d.)

Education, Minutes of the Committee of Council on, Parliamentary Papers, 1842, Vol. XXXIII

Eliot, George, *Adam Bede*, Everyman's Library (London, 1960)

——, *Brother Jacob*, Warwick Edition (Edinburgh and London, 1901)

——, 'English Peasants', *Westminster Review*, New Series, Vol. X (1 July 1856)

——, *Silas Marner*, Warwick Edition (Edinburgh and London, 1901)

Employment of Women and Children in Agriculture, Reports of Special Assistant Poor Law Commissioners on the, Parliamentary Papers, 1843, Vol. XII

Farington, Joseph, *The Farington Diary*, ed. James Greig, 8 vols (London, 1922-28)

Food riots, MSS. on, at Public Record Office, H.O.42/34, f.280

Fremantle, Anne (ed.), *The Wynne Diaries 1789-1820*, World's Classics (London, 1952)

Gaskell, Elizabeth C., *Mary Barton* (1848), Knutsford edn (London, 1906)

——, *The Life of Charlotte Brontë*, World's Classics (London, 1961)

——, *Wives and Daughters*, World's Classics (London, 1936)

Gentleman's Magazine, The, 1785, 1801 and 1811

Glyde, John, Jr, *Suffolk in the Nineteenth Century* (London, 1856)

Goldsmith, Oliver, *She Stoops to Conquer* in *Collected Works of Oliver Goldsmith*, ed. Arthur Friedman, 5 vols (Oxford, 1966)

——, *The Deserted Village* (1770) in *A Book of English Poetry*, ed. G.B. Harrison (Harmondsworth, 1968)

——, *The Vicar of Wakefield* in *Collected Works of Oliver Goldsmith*, ed. Arthur Friedman, 5 vols (Oxford, 1966)

Greville, Charles, *The Greville Memoirs*, eds Lytton Strachey and Roger Fulford, 8 vols (London, 1938)

Gunning, Henry, *Reminiscences of the University, Town, and County of Cambridge from the Year 1780*, 2 vols (London, 1854)

Hansard, 3rd Series, Vol. 87 (1846)

Hardy, Mary, *Mary Hardy's Diary*, ed. B. Cozens-Hardy (Norfolk Record Society, 1968)

Hazlitt, William, *The Spirit of the Age*, Everyman's Library (London, 1955)

Hood, Thomas, *Miscellaneous Uncollected Poems, 1821-1945* in *The Complete Poetical Works of Thomas Hood*, ed. Walter Jerrold, Oxford Edition (London, Edinburgh, Glasgow, 1906)

Howitt, William, *The Rural Life of England*, 2 vols (London, 1838)

Hyams, Edward (ed.), *Taine's Notes on England* (London, 1957)

Jackson's Oxford Journal, 1795

Kingsley, Charles, *Alton Locke*, Everyman's Library (London, 1970)

——, *Yeast* (London, 1925 ed.)

Lloyd's Evening Post, 14-16 June 1762

Lucas MSS at Bedfordshire Record Office, L.30/11/215, f.86 and 109

Marshall, William, *On the Appropriation and Inclosure of Commonable and Intermixed Lands* (London, 1801)

——, *On the Landed Property of England* (London, 1804)

Martineau, Harriet, *Forest and Game-Law Tales*, 3 vols (London, 1846)

Mayett, Joseph, *Autobiography of*, MS. at Buckinghamshire Record Office, D/X371

Mitford, Mary Russell, *Our Village*, 5 vols (London, 1824-1832)

Olmsted, Frederick Law, *Walks and Talks of an American Farmer* (Ann Arbor, 1967)

Olney, R.J., *Lincolnshire Politics 1832-1885* (Oxford, 1973)

Osbaldeston, George, *Squire Osbaldeston: His Autobiography*, ed. E.D. Cuming (London, 1926)

'Paston, George' [Emily M. Symonds], *Sidelights on the Georgian Period* (London, 1902)

Peacock, Thomas Love, *Crotchet Castle* (Harmondsworth, 1982)

Poor Law Report of 1834, The, eds S.G. and E.O.A. Checkland (Harmondsworth, 1974)

Roberts, William, *Memoirs of the Life and Correspondence of Mrs. Hannah More*, 2nd edn, 4 vols (London, 1834)

Saint-Fond, B. Faujas, *Travels in England, Scotland and the Hebrides*, 2 vols (London, 1799)

Shelley, Percy Bysshe, *Selected Poems*, World's Classics (London, 1960)
Skinner, John, *Journal of a Somerset Rector 1803-1834*, eds Howard and Peter Coombs (London and New York, 1984)
Surtees, R.S., *Ask Mamma*, Folio Society ed. 1954
——, *Handley Cross* (London, 1930)
——, *Mr. Sponge's Sporting Tour*, World's Classics (London, 1958)
Tennyson, Alfred, *The Poems of Tennyson*, ed. Christopher Ricks (London, 1969)
Thirsk, Joan and Imray, Jean (eds), *Suffolk Farming in the Nineteenth Century* (Suffolk Record Society, 1958)
Trollope, Anthony, *Barchester Towers*, World's Classics (London, 1960)
——, *Framley Parsonage*, World's Classics (London, 1957)
——, *The Small House at Allington*, World's Classics (London, 1959)
Trollope, Mrs Frances, *Jessie Phillips* (London, 1844)
Walpole, Horace, *The Yale Edition of Horace Walpole's Correspondence*, ed. W.S. Lewis et al., Vol. 38 (of 48 vols) (London, 1974)
Wesley, John, *The Journal of*, ed. Nehemiah Curnock, 8 vols (London, 1909)
White, Gilbert, *The Natural History of Selborne* (1789), Everyman's Library (London, 1949)
Woodforde, James, *The Diary of a Country Parson 1758-1802*, ed. John Beresford, World's Classics (London, 1967)
Wordsworth, William, *The Poetical Works*, ed. E. de Selincourt, 5 vols (Oxford, 1952)
——, *The Prelude* in *The Poetical Works of William Wordsworth*, ed. Thos Hutchinson (London, 1904)
Wrekington Hiring in *Collection of Broadsides, etc.* at British Library, 1875. d.13
Young, Arthur, *A Six Weeks' Tour Through the Southern Counties of England and Wales* (London, 1768)
——, MSS at the British Library, Add. MSS 35,129, f.78

Secondary Sources

The following list includes a selection of books on the economic, social and literary history of the later Georgian and early Victorian period. For the most part, these are general surveys only, designed to amplify or explain the broad theme of the book, rather than detailed studies of specialised topics within the period covered.

Ashton, T.S., *An Economic History of England: The 18th Century* (London, 1972)

Bettey, J.H., *Rural Life in Wessex 1500-1900* (Bradford-on-Avon, 1977)

Bohstedt, John, *Riots and Community Politics in England and Wales 1790-1810* (Cambridge, Mass., 1983)

Bovill, E.W., *English Country Life 1780-1830* (London, 1962)

——, *The England of Nimrod and Surtees 1815-1854* (London, 1959)

Chambers, J.D. and Mingay, G.E., *The Agricultural Revolution 1750-1880* (London, 1966)

Deane, Phyllis and Cole, W.A., *British Economic Growth 1688-1959* (Cambridge, 1964)

Duckworth, Alistair M., *The Improvement of the Estate: A Study of Jane Austen's Novels* (Baltimore and London, 1971)

Fuller, Margaret, *West Country Friendly Societies* (Reading, 1964)

Hammond, J.L. and Barbara, *The Village Labourer*, Guild Books, 2 vols (London, 1948)

Hay, Douglas, Linebaugh, Peter, and Thompson, E.P. (eds), *Albion's Fatal Tree* (London, 1975)

Hobsbawm, E.J. and Rudé, George, *Captain Swing* (London, 1969)

Holderness, B.A., ' "Open" and "Close" Parishes in England in the Eighteenth and Nineteenth Centuries', *Agricultural History Review*, Vol. XX (1972)

Horn, Pamela, *The Rural World 1780-1850* (London, 1980)

Jones, E.L., *The Development of English Agriculture 1815-1873* (London, 1968)

Keith, W.J., *The Rural Tradition* (Hassocks, 1975)

Kerr, Barbara, *Bound to the Soil* (London, 1968)

Malcolmson, Robert W., *Popular Recreations in English Society 1700-1850* (Cambridge, 1973)

Martin, J.M., 'Village Traders and the Emergence of a Proletariat in South Warwickshire, 1750-1851', *Agricultural History Review*, Vol. XXXII (1984)

Mathias, Peter, *The First Industrial Nation*, 2nd edn (London, 1983)

Mingay, G.E., *English Landed Society in the Eighteenth Century* (London, 1963)

——, *The Gentry* (London and New York, 1976)

——, ed., *The Victorian Countryside*, 2 vols (London, 1981)

Patterson, Clara Burdett, *Angela Burdett-Coutts and the Victorians* (London, 1953)

Peacock, A.J., *Bread or Blood* (London, 1965)
Pinchbeck, Ivy, *Women Workers and the Industrial Revolution 1750-1850* (London, 1930)
Rich, Eric E., *The Education Act, 1870* (London, 1970)
Rose, Michael E., *The English Poor Law 1780-1930* (Newton Abbot, 1971)
Sales, Roger, *English Literature in History: Pastoral and Politics 1780-1830* (London, 1983)
Spring, David, 'A Great Agricultural Estate: Netherby under Sir James Graham, 1820-1845', in *Agricultural History*, Vol. 29 (1955)
——, *The English Landed Estate in the Nineteenth Century: Its Administration* (Baltimore, 1963)
Stone, Lawrence and Stone, Jeanne C. Fawtier, *An Open Elite? England 1540-1880* (Oxford, 1984)
Thompson, F.M.L., *English Landed Society in the Nineteenth Century* (London, 1963)
Turberville, A.S. (ed.), *Johnson's England*, 2 vols (Oxford, 1965)
Turner, Michael, *Enclosure in Britain 1750-1830* (London, 1984)
——, 'Parliamentary Enclosure and Landownership Change in Buckinghamshire', *Economic History Review*, 2nd Series, Vol. XXVIII (November, 1975)
Watson, Frederick, *Robert Smith Surtees* (London, 1933)
Williams, Raymond, *Culture and Society 1780-1950* (Harmondsworth, 1982)
——, *The Country and the City* (London, 1973)

Index